Lessons from Ephesians

A 12-week study into the practical applications

of Paul's epistle to the Ephesians

Tracey S. Dowdy

To my husband Roy. Outside my salvation, you are God's most perfect gift to me.

Table of Contents

Introduction	1
Chapter 1 - The Blessing of Salvation	13
Chapter 2 - Prayer of Thanksgiving	24
Chapter 3 - From Death to Life	35
Chapter 4 - Welcome to the Family	46
Chapter 5 - God's Mystery Revealed	57
Chapter 6 - Power and Love	67
Chapter 7 - Christian Maturity	77
Chapter 8 - True Transformation	88
Chapter 9 - Walk This Way	99
Chapter 10 - Spirit-Led Relationships	111
Chapter 11 - Suit Up!	126
Conclusion	139
Acknowledgments	142
Sources	146

Introduction

When telling a story or unraveling a mystery, I've often found that the beginning, as they say, is the best place to start. Context clues are essential to understanding the nuances of language and subtext of the illustrations used. This is particularly important when studying Scripture. "Proof texting" can take Bible verses out of context to support an argument which inevitably leads to warped conclusions and false theology. The Bible is God-breathed, written across centuries by people led by the Holy Spirit to record what they observed, every word inspired and intentional.

So as we unpack Paul's epistle to the Ephesians, we need to go back to the questions we learned to ask in elementary school: who, what, when, where, and why. Who was the Apostle Paul? What is an epistle? When was Ephesians written? Where was Paul when he wrote this epistle? Why is studying Ephesians so important for the follower of Christ?

WHO was the Apostle Paul?

The apostle Paul was born in Tarsus, modern-day Tersous, in southeastern Turkey. It was a free city and a place of learning and Hellenistic culture fusing the ancient Greek world with Western Asia, Northeastern Africa, and Southwestern Asia.

In the Book of Acts, we learn Paul was known by his Hebrew name Saul until Acts 13:9. He was educated from boyhood in Jerusalem (Acts 22:3), trained as a rabbi, yet earned his living as a tentmaker. Paul was intelligent, scholarly, and spoke at least three languages. He was also a leading figure in the persecution of Christians in the years following Jesus' crucifixion and saw his mission as Pharisee as nothing less than the preservation and protection of Judaism. His conversion story is one of the most dramatic recorded in Scripture.

While traveling 150 miles from Jerusalem to Damascus, he had a supernatural encounter with the risen Jesus. Saul's conversion from devout Jew, persecuting Christ-followers to devout Christian, fearlessly spreading the gospel despite imprisonment and frequent opposition, is recorded three separate times in Acts (Acts 9, Acts 22, Acts 26). The conversion of Saul-the- Zealot and his transformation into Paul the apostle showed the world that Jesus intended the gospel for both Jews and Gentiles. This demonstration was intended to override any argument from the early Jewish Christians who believed that the gospel was for them alone.

Paul's ministry spanned thirty-five years from his conversion in AD 33 to his death in 68, during which time he helped establish Christianity as a new religion rather than simply a sect of Judaism. Paul traveled extensively while preaching the gospel to the Gentiles. His ministry included the assertion that the gospel was for both Jew and Gentile and that non-Jewish disciples of Christ had freedom from Jewish law.

Paul teaches in such a way that both his Jewish and Gentile audiences would understand as he was well-qualified to be the apostle to both audiences. Having been trained in Mosaic Law under Gamaliel (Acts 22:3) and having received a classical Roman education in Tarsus, Paul could argue his points based on his knowledge of Jewish Law (Galatians 4:21–31) and use illustrations from Greek literature (Acts 17:28; Titus 1:12; 1 Corinthians 15:33) to further illustrate his teaching.

His boldness in sharing the gospel was met with frequent opposition. Paul was arrested and jailed on three different occasions, enduring the full spectrum of treatment in Roman jails. Though we don't know the manner of Paul's death, we do know that he was ready to meet the Savior he so loved and served. In Philippians 1:21-24, he proclaimed, "For to me, to live is Christ and to die is gain. If I am to go on living in the body, this will mean fruitful labor for me. Yet what shall I choose? I do not know! I am torn between the two: I desire to depart and be with Christ, which is better by far, but it is more necessary for you that I remain in the body."

WHAT is an Epistle?

An epistle is a form of correspondence common in Paul's day that was most often written by individuals regarded as teachers or leaders and viewed as directive and authoritative. . Our English word "epistle" is derived from the Greek word epistolé, meaning "letter," "message," or "dispatch." In Hebrew, the word is "iggerah," also meaning "letter," and is primarily used for missives—lengthy, official, formal letters from someone in a position of authority.

Of the 27 books in the New Testament, 21 are epistles, and of these, 13 were written by Paul. Though initially intended for a specific audience, these 21 epistles contain instruction intended to help fellow believers grow in their faith that remains relevant today.

Though the structure of an epistle varies between authors, it typically follows a common template. The author begins with a personal greeting identifying him or herself and the intended recipient(s) (Ephesians 1:1) and often speaks a blessing over them (Ephesians 1:2). The author then dives into the issues to be addressed.

In writing to the church at Ephesus, Paul breaks from this model to praise God for His abundant blessings and thanks Him for the gift of salvation and reconciliation through Christ. He also pauses to commend the Ephesians for their testimony and love for others. Finally, he prays for them to grow in their faith and for continued recognition of Christ's authority through His resurrection and exaltation.

Many New Testament epistles contain admonitions to turn away from sinful practices and instructions on how to live as a follower of Christ (Ephesians 4-5). If the epistle is addressed to a church (Ephesians, Philippians, Colossians) rather than an individual (Timothy, Philemon), then the prayer functions as a benediction.

Finally, an epistle concludes with the writer offering any final instructions and a farewell to his or her readers. In the New Testament epistles, if the letter is addressed to a church (Ephesians, Philippians, Colossians) rather than an individual (Timothy, Philemon), then typically, a prayer functions as a benediction and conclusion to the epistle. For example, Paul ends Ephesians with an admonition to put on the full armor of God and asks for prayer for himself and other believers. He also sends his love and prayers for grace and peace to those that love God (Ephesians 6:10-24).

WHEN was Ephesians written?

Paul writes his epistle in AD 60 to the church in Ephesus, an ancient port city near the western shores of modern-day Turkey. Once considered the most important Greek city and trading center in the Mediterranean region, its ruins are well preserved and the source of significant archaeological finds. At the time of Paul's writing, Ephesus was the fourth largest city in the Western world, boasting a population of approximately 250,000 people. Only Rome, Alexandria, and Antioch were larger. It was critically important for political reasons and served as the capital of the Roman province of Asia Minor.

Paul wrote to the Ephesians at a time in history when the city of Ephesus was a religious epicenter for pagan worshipers of the goddess Artemis. The Temple of Artemis was located in the heart of the city and was a focal point of culture, religion, and commerce. Archeological research reveals that Ephesus was considered the "nurturer" of Artemis. The goddess, in turn, was said to have made Ephesus the most "glorious" city in the entire province of Asia. Recognized as one of the Seven Wonders of the Ancient World, the temple is believed to have been the largest building in the world at that time, estimated to be four times larger than the Parthenon. Measuring 200 feet wide by 400 feet long, the temple featured 127 columns, many of which were overlaid with pure gold, standing 60 feet tall to support its massive roof. This lavish worship of Artemis plays an important role in Paul's ministry as he looked for every opportunity to share the gospel through avenues such as an annual festival in Artemis' honor that brought up to half a million worshippers to Ephesus every year.

Paul spent three years in Ephesus, allowing him insight into the culture and hearts of its people. In response to his preaching and miracles, Ephesus became a hotbed of evangelism for the early church. In fact, the Ephesian Christians burned so many books about the occult and magic that the value was equivalent to nearly 140 years' pay for the average laborer (Acts 19:18-19). It is no wonder that Demetrius, a silversmith who minted coins featuring the likeness of

Artemis, was so infuriated over Paul's influence on the city that he incited a riot (Acts 19:24–25). Nevertheless, Ephesian officials protected Paul and his followers, and eventually, Christianity became the official religion of Ephesus during the Byzantine era (395 CE—1453) under Constantine the Great.

Ephesus endured multiple attacks by invading armies, frequently changing rulers between conquerors. The city relied heavily on its harbor for commerce and trade, but the constant accumulation of silt caused it to deteriorate until Ephesus became a port city without a port. A massive earthquake in the sixth and seventh centuries reduced Ephesus to a shell of its former self. These factors, coupled with Arab invasions, ultimately hastened the city's decline. By the end of the 15th century, the once magnificent city of Ephesus was abandoned.

WHERE was Paul when he wrote Ephesians?

Paul wrote to the Ephesians from a Roman prison while under house arrest. Jewish leaders wrongly assumed he had brought a Gentile into an area of the temple Gentiles were forbidden to enter. A riot ensued, and Paul was arrested (Acts 21:27-36).

At the time of his incarceration, Paul was placed in an uncertain situation where he might be jailed for an extended period. However, this time of unrest and political riots in Roman history ultimately lent itself to Paul having time to write to his followers while on house arrest.

The criminal justice system in Rome drastically differed from what we are accustomed to today in the United States. Rome had no police force; its people were expected to police themselves, though soldiers were stationed outside the city to maintain order. An ever-present threat of riots existed as political unrest simmered just under the surface. From its founding as The First Republic, Rome's leadership treated accused criminals ruthlessly. In Paul's day, Rome was still a military-based society in an era of marked brutality. Torture and capital punishment were the norms, and incarceration in Roman prisons was rarely long-term. Much depended on the social status of the accused and the specific offense with which they were charged. Punishments ranged from a monetary fine to forced labor on public projects, exile, or execution.

As most prisoners were awaiting trial or execution, the length of their prison term usually depended on how swiftly a trial date could be set and carried out. Long-term incarceration was not a legally sanctioned punishment, though there were exceptions. For example, debtors would often languish in jail until friends or family could pay their debt, and accused individuals in outlying Roman provinces faced indefinite incarceration as they had to wait for a judge to come to town. Moreover, imprisoned political figures sometimes found the justice system could be manipulated with bribes in their opponent's favor, leaving them languishing in jail.

Once a verdict had been reached, judgment was swift, leading some condemned prisoners to choose suicide over execution by the court. Executions were usually barbaric, with the condemned suffering such agonizing fates as being buried or burned alive, impaled, or crucified, sometimes upside down. One particularly gruesome fate was reserved for those who committed patricide. The prisoner would be bound, then sewn into a heavy sack with a snake, a rooster, a monkey, and a dog. The sack would then be thrown into a river.

Paul endured the full spectrum of conditions beginning with his arrest in Acts 16:23-30, where he was chained in a common holding cell in Philippi. He experienced better conditions during his imprisonment, recorded in Acts 23:35 when he was held in Herod's Praetoria in Caesarea for two years as he awaited his trial. His final imprisonment found him under house arrest in Rome, where he writes his five prison epistles, including his letter to the Ephesians (Acts 28:16). As a Roman citizen, he lived in relative comfort while under house arrest, though he was guarded around the clock by soldiers of the elite Praetorian Guard and most likely chained to his jailer.

Paul would have been responsible for maintaining himself during his imprisonment,

including providing his own food and clothing, which his followers graciously supplied (Philippians 4:14-18).

WHY is studying Ephesians important?

One could argue that the entire canon of Scripture is contained in Ephesians. From Genesis through

Revelation, God lays out His redemptive plan for humanity fulfilled in Jesus Christ.

In Ephesians, Paul demonstrates that through God's redemptive plan—Jesus' sacrifice—God and man are reconciled, and God is at work in our redemption to build His church. We are no longer bound by Old Testament Law but are reconciled to God through His gift of salvation.

Ephesians is a study of how the Church is not merely a location; it is our identity as followers of Christ. Paul emphasizes the importance of God's work in the individual believer's life and His work as a body of believers—His Church (Ephesians 1:3-14). It is a master class on God's gifts to us that enable us to walk in holiness, discernment, and love as we take part in the spiritual warfare all around us.

At its heart, Ephesians is the story of God's glory, His grace, and His fulfilled promise of redemption to all humanity. The Jewish people, whom God named as His chosen people, were promised a Messiah. This covenant between God and His people was fulfilled by Jesus Christ. Jewish people were the earliest to accept the gospel (Ephesians 1:11), which then spread to Gentiles (Ephesians 1:13). The Ephesian believers were among the first Gentile converts of Paul's ministry (Acts 18:18–19).

Ephesians reminds us that our hope is found in Jesus Christ. In Him, we have redemption, forgiveness, and we are adopted into the family of God. This grants us access to abundant spiritual blessings found only in heavenly places (Ephesians 1:3-12). Paul wants us to remember that Jesus is the answer to every problem and the source of true joy. Ephesians also reminds us that our sinful nature doesn't miraculously vanish at the moment of our salvation (Ephesians 4:22). Paul identifies our real enemy - Satan (Ephesians 6:12). God's grace resurrects us to new life in Him. Because our life and identity are now in Him, we are united because we have one Father (Ephesians 4:2-6).

Pulling together the answers to these questions, we begin to see how Paul weaves a tapestry with a singular scarlet thread running from beginning to end. Ephesians presents the gospel of Jesus Christ as the answer to the brokenness around us. The problems of this world—racism, oppression, greed, injustice—are all sourced from the problem of sin and the fallen nature of the human heart. We need social justice and reform, but Ephesians shows us the gospel is the only way to see true transformation in the world.

Ephesians is an invitation from God to be the gospel to a lost and dying world, a living testimony of God's glory and grace. It is an invitation from God to discover who He desires us to be, what He created us to do, and what we have in Christ. As followers of Christ, we are to be the gospel to a lost and dying world, a living testimony of God's glory and grace.

Chapter 1 - The Blessing of Salvation

Ephesians 1:1-14

The Marianas Trench, located on the western North Pacific Ocean floor, east of the Philippines and the Mariana Islands, is a crescent-shaped geological depression averaging more than 1,500 miles (2,550 kilometers) long and 43 miles (69 kilometers) wide. It is the deepest such trench known on earth, with its deepest point, Challenger Deep, estimated to have a depth of almost 11,000 km (7 miles). To put that in perspective, if Mount Everest (8,848 km or 5.5 miles) were dropped into the Marianas Trench, its peak would still be more than a mile (1.6 km) underwater.

Scientists have struggled to measure the exact depth of Challenger Deep from the surface. Water pressure at the bottom of the trench is a crushing eight tons per square inch—or about a thousand times what we experience at sea level, making exploration difficult. Scientists agree there is still much to be covered as they continue to dive deeper into its mysteries.

Ephesians, like the Marianas Trench, is both deep and wide. Theologians and scholars have studied it for centuries, and like all Scripture, it continues to intrigue and enlighten us as we explore its mysteries. Chapter one alone references subjects as profound as our salvation, the mystery of God's will, predestination, adoption as sons and daughters of God, and the sealing of the Holy Spirit.

Years earlier, Paul wrote to the Corinthians believers, "However, as it is written: 'What no eye has seen, what no ear has heard, and what no human mind has conceived'—the things God has prepared for those who love him—these are the things God has revealed to us by his Spirit" (1 Corinthians 2:9-10). Ephesians embodies these verses, revealing all God has prepared for those who love Him.

Paul opens his letter to the Ephesians by introducing himself to the reader (Ephesians 1:1-2), though debate exists regarding the letter's intended audience. Some scholars insist Ephesians was written as a circular letter intended for any Christians who might read it. In contrast, others argue it was meant for a specific audience, with personal greetings later omitted for general use. Questions surrounding his intended audience aside, Paul identifies himself as an apostle of Jesus Christ, granting him authority to speak to issues of faith and the conduct of the church.

Paul then commends the faithfulness of the Ephesian believers. This praise is notable because they lived in a culture entrenched in the worship of Artemis (not to be confused with the Greek goddess Artemis who was a huntress), the goddess of fertility who was the most worshiped goddess in Asia at the time. Known as the "Queen of Heaven," "Savior," and "Mother Goddess," hundreds of eunuch priests, virgin priestesses, and religious prostitutes served Artemis at her Ephesian temple. Followers worshipped Artemis through erotic rituals that combined dancing, singing, dramatic productions, and chanting their allegiance. Countless people were drawn to the cult with its promise of fertility, long life, sexual fulfillment, and protection during pregnancy and childbirth.

Paul's epistle reflects his relationship and ministry to the believers in Ephesus. Paul refrained from deriding and antagonizing Artemis' followers, choosing instead to preach the gospel and let its life-changing power be the culture-changer rather than shaming and attacking. When Demetrius the silversmith tried to incite a riot against him and his ministry, the Ephesian city clerk said, "These men (Christians)...are neither sacrilegious nor blasphemers of our goddess...there is no cause that we can give to justify this commotion" (Acts 19:27; 40).

Instead, Paul chose to preach the gospel and let its life-changing power be the culture-changer. The testimony of these Ephesian believers demonstrated that "God did not send His Son into the world to condemn the world, but to save the world through Him" (John 3:17). They allowed the Holy Spirit to radically transform them, and this pursuit of Christlikeness led to a new way of thinking, believing, and behaving. Their lifestyle stood in stark contrast to those who worshiped Artemis, boldly burning their books on magic and spell casting and choosing to find sexual fulfillment in marriage rather than with temple prostitutes. It is no wonder Paul applauds their faithfulness and extends God's grace and peace to the Christians in Ephesus.

With his authority established, Paul pauses to express his gratitude for God's blessings anchored in Christ and in the heavenly places (Ephesians 1:3). He leaves no doubt about who we are and whose we are (v.4-5). Once we were God's enemies, now we are reconciled to Him through His Son, set apart, anchored in Christ through His work in salvation.

These first verses in Ephesians echo King David's words in Psalm 103. There, God calls us to trust Him as we navigate this fallen world. God has chosen us, blessed us, saved us, made His purpose known to us, and reconciled us to Him.

Ephesians 1:3-14 is one sentence in Greek. In English, that's a run-on sentence, making it difficult to read, so translators have broken it down into more easily understandable verses. However, recognizing these verses form a single sentence helps us decode Paul's message and see it as one thought: we are blessed with spiritual riches from God the Father (Ephesians 1:4-6), from the Son (Ephesians 1:7-12), and the Holy Spirit (Ephesians 1:13-14).

Beginning in Ephesians 1:3-4, Paul brings up one of the most complex and debated topics among theologians. Entire Christian denominations have been birthed from these debates, with both sides emphatic they have interpreted Scripture as God intended. What issue could be so contentious? Predestination. Volume after volume of scholarly treatises have been written, countless sermons preached, and interpretations hotly contested.

I have never been a great athlete. It is more accurate to say that I've never been an athlete. Though I wasn't always last when it came time to pick teams in gym class, it wasn't unusual to hear, "Fine. I'll take Tracey, and you get Carrie." If you need someone to stand on the sidelines and toss out color commentary, I'm your girl. If you need someone to get the puck in the net or throw that game-winning touchdown, get ready to settle for a participation ribbon.

I've heard predestination oversimplified using the analogy of God picking teams in gym class. In reality, that reduces the intent of an omnipotent God who imbued humanity with free will to a middle schooler trying to triumph on the dodgeball court. Instead, predestination in Scripture is a picture of a loving God who predestined humanity for adoption as sons and daughters because He desired a relationship with us and so that His grace would be enjoyed and magnified through Jesus Christ, "in accordance with his pleasure and will" (Ephesians 1:5) and to the praise of his glorious grace (Ephesians 1:6). God chose us, lest there be any debate surrounding the basis of our salvation. Through Christ, we become His sons and daughters, the church; "a chosen people, a royal priesthood, a holy nation, God's special possession, that you may declare the praises of him who called you out of darkness into his wonderful light" (1 Peter 2:9). All glory and praise belong to Him for the blessing of our salvation, born out of God's desire for fellowship with us, His fallen creation. God alone loves, redeems, and restores.

For all its deep theology, Ephesians is, at its heart, a profoundly practical book. Paul reminds his readers that our salvation in Christ is an act of God. Jesus died, and He bled for our forgiveness (Ephesians 1:7). This act was part of the redemptive process by which we are no longer slaves to our sinful nature but are raised to new life in our redeemer. Salvation is a gift - not a reward for good work. Some believe that salvation may be earned through good works; however, Scripture is clear that all have sinned, and sin separates us from God (Romans 3:9-12; 23).

We are in Christ, and we have been given the mind of Christ. Paul uses the phrase "in Him" or "in Christ" eight times; reference to "His" is used nine times; and "He," "God," or "Jesus" is the subject used eight times. Why? Because Paul wants us to remember that we can call ourselves Christians or "God's holy people" (v. 1), but not because of some herculean effort on our part. It is only by grace we have been saved, through faith—not of ourselves, it is a gift from God—not by works we have done, so that no one can boast. (Ephesians 2:8-9). Living the Christian life is impossible apart from God. All the follower of Christ can do is "[hear] the word of truth," "[believe]" and "put our hope in Christ." Every blessing is anchored in Christ's work, salvation, and heavenly places (v.3).

It is equally as foolish for us to claim credit for our salvation as it would be for a child to claim the credit for their Christmas presents because they unwrapped and opened them. The child didn't shop for the presents, work to pay for them, wrap them or put them under the tree. The child simply accepted the gifts that were presented. Only when the gift was accepted did it truly become their own. God offers His gift of salvation, but for us to be saved, we must accept that gift. If we want to enjoy every spiritual blessing that comes from being claimed, chosen, marked, predestined, and forgiven by God, we must accept God's gift of salvation. It is all for God, to His glory, and for His praise, and rightly so. Rather than glory in our own self-righteousness, we should instead be humbled and rejoice that we have been adopted as sons and daughters by God our Father.

Paul's use of the phrase "adoption to sonship" (v.5) would have had particular meaning for his Ephesian audience. Under Roman law, adopted children were granted the same rights and privileges as natural-born children, even if they had been born into slavery. They became equal heirs, regarded as new people with a new life in their new families. Furthermore, their former life was completely wiped out, and all debts were canceled. They were in a new relationship with new families. By asserting that we are adopted to sonship through our salvation, Paul eliminates any doubt about who we are and Whose we are.

"Redemption" is the price paid to free an enslaved person. Through salvation, we are no longer slaves to sin but free to walk in new life (Romans 6:1-7). We have freedom from the wrath of God, the curse of the law by which we had been bound. "For you have not received a spirit of slavery leading to fear again, but you have received a spirit of adoption as sons by which we cry out, 'Abba! Father!'" (Romans 8:15).

Paul repeatedly expresses his gratitude that God has made known to us what was once a mystery, namely His plan of salvation to bring all of creation to unity under Christ. (v.9-10). Paul uses the term "mystery" several times in his letters. In Colossians 1:27, he wrote, "To them God has chosen to make known among the Gentiles the glorious riches of this mystery, which is Christ in you, the hope of glory." What is this mystery? The secret of our salvation, hidden during the Old Testament, is revealed in the New Testament in Jesus Christ.

God's intention and plan for salvation is for Jews and Gentiles to be united in one body with Christ as the head. God wasn't manipulating or deliberately hiding His plan of salvation in the Old Testament, but His plan couldn't be understood until after Jesus' death, burial, and resurrection. Still today, though, many do not accept Him as Savior. But all will come to terms with the supremacy of Jesus, as Paul writes in Philippians 2:10-11, one day, at the name of Jesus, every knee will bow, in heaven and on earth and under the earth, and every tongue will acknowledge that Jesus Christ is Lord, to the glory of God the Father.

Paul wants his readers to remember that God is sovereign and planned to redeem us from before the moment of creation. He is sovereign; He is in control.

So even when our lives seem chaotic, uncertain, and overwhelming, we can take comfort in knowing that our heavenly father sees, understands, and cares. Nothing Satan throws at us is beyond God's power to defeat, and no failure is so great that it is beyond His power to redeem.

One of the greatest promises in all of Scripture is found in Ephesians 1:13-14. Paul writes, "...you also were included in Christ when you heard the message of truth, the gospel of your salvation. When you believed, you were marked in him with a seal, the promised Holy Spirit." This is perhaps the most significant of all the blessings of salvation Paul has listed for us in Ephesians 1.

The word Paul uses for "guarantee" is a word that is used in reference to financial transactions. Think of it like this: if I bought a car from a dealership, I'd pay a certain amount as a down payment, standing as a guarantee that the full amount would be paid later. The Holy Spirit is our "down payment," part of the promised future that has come to meet us here in the present.

Like a signature on a contract, the Holy Spirit in us proves we are God's own children, seals our salvation, and secures eternal life. However, his work in us is but a shadow of the complete transformation we will experience in eternity.

And that changes everything.

Discussion Questions

1. What is a "spiritual blessing" according to Ephesians 1:3?

2. Five spiritual blessings that God has given to His people are listed in these verses. Name and give a simple definition or description for each one.

3. Why is a condemnation of the lost and their lifestyle a poor evangelical tool?

4. Paul writes to the Ephesians that we have been foreordained, predestined to be sons and daughters of God.

   a. Does that mean those who aren't believers in Christ have not been pre-chosen to be in a relationship with God?

   b. If God knows some are destined for hell, why doesn't he intervene and save them? What role does free will play in all of this?

5. How does knowing you were chosen before the foundation of the world help you deal with past failures and mistakes and encourage you about your future?

6. Paul concludes this section by explaining how practical the knowledge of these spiritual blessings can be. As your eyes are opened to all that you have in Christ, what is the result in your life?

Chapter 2 - Prayer of Thanksgiving

Ephesians 1:15-23

Over the years, many of my American friends have been surprised to discover Canadians celebrate Thanksgiving too. Of course, it is not on the same scale as what we do here in the United States. To be fair, it isn't easy to compete with the scale of an American holiday.

The Indigenous peoples of Canada celebrated the fall harvest before European settlers set foot in North America. First Nations across Turtle Island have long given thanks for surviving winter and for receiving crops and game as a reward for their hard work. Rituals include prayer, feasting, dancing, potlatch (potluck), and other ceremonies varying among the people giving thanks.

In 1578, British explorer Martin Frobisher hosted a "Thanksgiving meal" in gratitude to God for allowing his ship safe passage through northern North America. He and his crew sat down to a lavish feast—if you consider salt beef, biscuits, and mushy peas lavish—giving thanks through Communion for their safe arrival in what was then Newfoundland. Now accepted as the first "Canadian" Thanksgiving, their celebration was forty-three years before the first "American" Thanksgiving, and almost three hundred years before Canada became a country. The first Canadian Thanksgiving after Confederation wasn't until April 1872, when Canadians celebrated the recovery of Queen Victoria's husband, the Prince of Wales, from a near-fatal illness.

While there are distinct differences—Canadians celebrate Thanksgiving on the second Monday in October instead of the third Thursday in November, and there's no Black Friday shopping frenzy—much is the same on both sides of the border. We gather with family and friends, (over)eat turkey and all the sides, watch football, and nap while the game plays in the background. Most importantly, the heartbeat of the holiday is the same on both sides of the border—gratitude for all that is good in our lives.

Though every holiday brings its share of stressors, Thanksgiving's focus on gratitude can mitigate negative emotions like sadness, anxiety, or depression the holidays may trigger. Studies show that gratitude is strongly and consistently associated with greater happiness and increased positive emotions. It can also improve your health, help manage stress, and build strong, lasting relationships. Who couldn't use a little more of that in their life?

Psychologists Dr. Robert A. Emmons of the University of California, Davis, and Dr. Michael E. McCullough of the University of Miami, have done extensive research on gratitude. In one study, they asked all participants to write a few sentences each week, focusing on specific topics.

Control Group A wrote about things during the week for which they were grateful. Control Group B wrote about daily irritations or something that had displeased them. Control Group C wrote about events that had affected them without emphasizing positive or negative experiences or events. After ten weeks had passed, they evaluated the results. Participants who wrote about gratitude were more optimistic, content, and felt better about their lives. They also exercised more and had fewer visits to physicians than those who focused on negative experiences or irritations.

Dr. Martin E. P. Seligman, a psychologist at the University of Pennsylvania, another leading gratitude researcher, tested the impact of positive psychological interventions on 411 people. In this test, each participant was asked to write about his or her early childhood memories. Their week's assignment was to write and personally deliver a letter of gratitude to an individual they had never properly thanked for his or her kindness; participants immediately exhibited a significant increase in their happiness scores, greater than any other intervention. Moreover, the beneficial impact of the letter and subsequent interaction with the recipient lasted for a month.

Paul understood the power of gratitude as evidenced throughout his prison epistles. In Philippians 4:12, he wrote, "I know what it is to be in need, and I know what it is to have plenty. I have learned the secret of being content in any and every situation, whether well fed or hungry, whether living in plenty or in want." Even though he was on house arrest in a Roman prison, a situation that would have most others praying for release, Paul focused on others knowing and living out the truth of the gospel. His prayers were filled with thanks for what God was doing among the believers in Ephesus.

Paul opens his letter to the Ephesians with encouragement and thanksgiving. He prays believers would understand who they are in Christ and describes the multitude of spiritual blessings in Him. Paul tells the Ephesians that he prays without ceasing, asking that God might give them a spirit of wisdom and revelation. "I have not stopped giving thanks for you, remembering you in my prayers" (v. 16).

Paul wants believers to spend time with God in prayer so the Jesus that walks through the gospel can walk alongside us, leading and guiding every step we take. That's why in Ephesians 1:15-23, Paul shares a prayer of thanksgiving in light of all that God has done for us in Christ Jesus (Ephesians 1:1-14). Remember that this prayer of gratitude follows the epic run-on sentence spanning verses 3-13, which he punctuates with thanksgiving in verses 6, 12, and 14. These opening verses tell the story of salvation, praise God's glory, and culminate with the good news of salvation and the redemption of God's people.

It is "for this reason" that Paul's heart is filled with gratitude. He rejoices in the work Christ did for us—the choosing, predestination, redemption, forgiveness, empowering of the Holy Spirit, and the faith response of the people who had heard the gospel of truth. Ever since Paul heard about the transformed lives of the people, he has "not stopped giving thanks for [them], remembering [them] in [his] prayer." (v.15).

First, we are chosen, adopted, redeemed, and sealed. Here in the second half of chapter one, Paul describes what God wants us to have and what He wants us to know.

Paul prays that believers would:

- Know God better

- Know the hope of God's calling

- Know the riches of God's inheritance

- Know the surpassing greatness of God's power

First and foremost, he prays for believers to know God better. How do you get to know someone? By spending time with him or her, of course. I know about Elizabeth II, the queen of England, but I don't *know* her. On the other hand, I know my husband very well because we've been together since college. I know how he likes his coffee, favorite foods, and vacation spots. I also know things only discernible when you know someone well, like when the joke he made wasn't a joke because, though his mouth is smiling, his eyes most certainly are not. I see what sends him into a tailspin, what he mourns as missed opportunities, what he's most proud of, and what he regrets.

"Know" isn't a reference to facts like there are 5,280 feet in a mile or that a chef's hat has precisely 100 pleats. It is much more profound. Paul wants us to know these things experientially because it is only when the eyes of our hearts are opened can we truly know and discern the things of God. So, Paul's prayer is not merely that they have more answers but that they know God better. It is less about answering questions and being articulate than knowing what God has called us to. He outlines what he wants them to learn in v.18-19.

If we want to know God the way Paul prays for us to know Him, we must spend time with Him. How do we do that? Begin by studying His word. Dive into the Gospels and see how He interacted with those He met. Listen to His message to the crowds when He fed the 5,000 (John 6:1-70) or His compassion-filled interaction with the woman at the well (John 4:4-54). Feel His agony as He prays in the garden the night before His crucifixion (Luke 22:39-48), and rejoice in His promise to return in victory over death and the grave once and for all (Luke 9:18-27). But don't stop there. Scripture allows us to know about Jesus; salvation enables us to know Him.

Paul demonstrates a discipline in his prayer life that is both effective and challenging for us as Christ-followers. Rather than praying for specific results, "Lord, help these believers to grow their faith," he prays that God will give them the Spirit of wisdom and revelation so that they will know God better and the hope to which this same God called them.

    Paul wants us to see the riches of God's glorious inheritance in His people, which can now be counted because of our adoption as sons and daughters through Jesus. (v. 17-19). As believers, we are co-heirs with Christ, adopted into God's family (Romans 8:16). Our inheritance is nothing less than the gift of salvation and eternity with God through our new birth in Christ. Elsewhere in Scripture, the Apostle Peter tells us that this inheritance will never perish. "He has given us new birth into a living inheritance that can never perish, spoil or fade—kept in heaven for you" (1 Peter 1:4). Paul's prayer is for the church to know and better understand our salvation and what God has done for us through Christ.

    Paul prays that we might know God's power (v.19). It is this same power that raised Christ from death to life, placing Him at the right hand of His father, "far above all rule and authority, power and dominion" (v. 20). It is the power that raised the man thrown on the bones of Elisha (1 Kings 13:21), that transforms us, filling our lungs with the breath of new life. Note Paul uses the word power twice here. The gospel is not merely an idea or a worldview but God's power at work in people. The ultimate manifestation of the power of God is seen in the resurrection of Jesus Christ. His triumph guarantees that God's people shall be exalted in and with Him. (1 Corinthians 6:14; 15:43; Philippians 3:21).

In verses 22 and 23, Paul tells us that Christ has been placed as head of the church, which is his body. Paul wants believers to know God's power - again, not know about it, but to understand it experientially - as the power that saves, sanctifies, and sustains us. Paul intentionally reminds the Ephesians (and us) that the church is the "the fullness of Him who fills everything in every way." The church is not intended to be a place but a gathering where the people of Christ can know Him better and the power of His resurrection. Experiencing this power cannot help but leave the believer filled to bursting with gratitude for all God has done and will continue to do through us.

The idea of the church as the body of Christ is mentioned several times in the New Testament (Romans 12:4-5; 1 Corinthians 12:12- 27). It is possible that Paul first encountered this metaphor when Jesus Himself referred to Paul's persecution of the church as persecuting Jesus Himself (Acts 9:4; 22:7; 26:14). The metaphor is a perfect example of the Supreme nature and position of Jesus Christ, and yet His heartfelt love for and connection to us. Jesus identifies so closely with his church so as to call it His body.

Through the miraculous indwelling of the Holy Spirit that gives us the mind of Christ

(1 Corinthians 2:16), we can discern who God is and where He is at work. As we know Him better, we begin to see the world as He sees it. We can make decisions based on His will rather than our plans and aspirations. Only by aligning our hearts with God our Father can we discern His will. Only then can we hear what He will

tell us and what He has called us to do or see what He will reveal as the future for which He has equipped us, one that will truly satisfy us and carry us home to Him.

Jesus is the center, provider, and source of every need. He is supreme, seated at the right hand of His Father, and is all-sufficient. May God give us the Spirit of wisdom and revelation so that we know him better. May He open the eyes of our hearts so that we may understand that glorious hope to which we are called, the riches of His glorious inheritance in His holy people, and His incomparably great power for all those who believe.

Discussion Questions

1.   Why do you think Paul gave thanks to the Lord hearing of the Ephesian Christians' faith in Jesus and their love for the saints?

2.   Faith should not be reduced to believing in God or accepting doctrine, but actively trusting in what God has done and a life lived in response to God's actions. Understanding this, can people "hear" your faith? Share an example.

3.   Paul's prayer illustrates that our prayers can be more than just a list of needs. Compare Paul's prayer in Ephesians 1:15-23 with the Lord's Prayer in Matthew 6:9-13. Do your prayers follow these models, or are they little more than a honey-do list for God?

4.   When you pray, what consumes your prayers? What do you pray most for yourself and others?

5.   Paul prays that the Ephesians would know the hope of following God's calling. In a world that seems without hope, how can we communicate that there is hope in receiving the calling of God for our lives?

Chapter 3 - From Death to Life

Ephesians 2:1-10

The Walking Dead, based on a comic book series created by Robert Kirkman with artist Tony Moore, is one of the most-watched cable television series in history. Set in a post-zombie-apocalypse, the gratuitously violent show features groups of people struggling to build new lives and survive in a world overrun with zombies, known on the show as "walkers."

For the most part, it is standard zombie lore - decaying walkers shuffle along, mindless, heartless, lifeless. Anyone who is bitten by a walker is then zombified. The "good" guys want to rebuild a civil society, the "bad" guys are focused on self-preservation and domination, and the walkers are singularly focused and slaves to their hunger. In a deviation from the usual horror tropes, *The Walking Dead* reveals that everyone carries the virus. When they die, regardless of whether or not they've been bitten, they too become reanimated corpses—no one is immune. It is a world of chaos, and because all of humanity is infected, even the "good" guys can expect no peace after death. The title is an obvious metaphor. *The Walking Dead* isn't just a reference to the zombies; it is a nod to the living as well.

Taking that metaphor further, characters carrying a virus that's already made them part of the living dead is a profound allegory for Christianity and original sin. Think that's a stretch? In one exchange, two characters are debating their next move after having to flee their farm, a place that had been a sanctuary. Standing on a desolate stretch of highway in rural Georgia, surrounded by abandoned cars and decomposing bodies, farmer Hershel urges Rick, a father, to flee to safety with his son. Rick challenges Hershel — the show's self-professed Christian— "You're a man of God. Have some faith." Hershel replies, "I can't profess to understand God's plan. Christ promised the resurrection of the dead. I just thought he had something a little different in mind."

Not so subtle after all, is it?

Because of Adam and Eve's disobedience in the Garden of Eden, all humanity has been infected by sin. Our state of spiritual dead-ness, that is, separation from life and fellowship with God (Genesis 2:16-17), contaminates our minds, corrupts our bodies, and defiles our spirit. Paul describes our spiritually dead state — or "zombified," if you will—in Ephesians 2:1-3. "As for you, you were dead in your transgressions and sins, in which you used to live when you followed the ways of this world and of the ruler of the kingdom of the air, the spirit who is now at work in those who are disobedient." We lived as the walking dead, gratifying the cravings of our flesh and following its desires and thoughts. We were, by nature, deserving of wrath, unable to see or understand the things of the Spirit, nor could we take the initiative to seek God.

Lazarus could no more take credit for raising himself from the dead (John 11:1–44) than we can claim any creditin our salvation. Our salvation and changed life are entirely due to God's grace in our lives. The Ephesians, who repented and turned to faith in Christ, experienced a radical transformation in their lives as evidenced by turning their backs on pagan and idolatrous practices. Paul's implication in these verses is that every believer's life has an evident change in direction once he or she is saved. If an individual claims to have surrendered his life to God, yet his life shows no evidence of repentance, then the sincerity of his decision comes into question.

Paul's tone changes in verse four to joyfully declaring our new reality. Paul spells out why God has "made us alive with Christ." We are not one of the walking dead because:

- He is great with love for us
- God is rich in mercy
- God wants to show us the incomparable riches of His grace

- God expresses kindness

This joyful new reality is made possible only 'but for' the grace of God. The word "but" is one of the most significant in Scripture. Over and over, the phrase "but God" cues us to the notion that what was once thought impossible is, in fact, possible because of who God is and all He has promised for us. In verse 4, Paul uses "but" to contrast our former way of life with our new life in Christ. We were all dead in sin, living under Satan's influence, thinking only of self-gratification. But. But God was merciful. He didn't leave us in this state. Instead, He sent Jesus, who "made us alive together with Christ" by His grace because of His great mercy. This is certainly joyous news.

In verses 5 and 8, Paul reminds us, "You have been saved by grace." In the original Greek, Paul uses a passive, perfect periphrastic (using longer wording) participle (an action word used to describe something) worth examining. By using the passive voice, he underscores how we are passive regarding our salvation. God's grace has accomplished our salvation, not we ourselves. His use of the perfect tense and periphrastic participle highlight the duration of our being saved. It was completed in the past and remains our reality into the future, making it an ongoing demonstration of the immeasurable riches of divine grace (v. 7).

Paul's words reinforce the magnitude of God's mercy, love, grace, and kindness, which have the power to transform our lives as believers. Likewise, his words contrast the difference between our ongoing state of salvation against non-Christians who remain dead in sin and under Satan's influence. It is important to note that Paul doesn't bring up the Ephesians' former idolatry or sinful past to shame them as Satan would. Instead, Paul wants to celebrate God's initiative and His work in their salvation. We were dead and "deserving of wrath" (v.3), but now, we are alive and "raised up with Christ and seated with Him in the heavenly realms in Christ Jesus" (v. 6). Paul focuses on their freedom in Christ. It is another example of the joyful new reality of life we have in our salvation.

The great tragedy for humanity is that, like the mindless zombies, many who are spiritually dead are unaware of their state, and stillothers are outright hostile. Some might argue, "I'm a good person. I give to charity and don't lie, cheat, or steal. I don't live in sin." But as Paul says, we are all living in sin, "gratifying the cravings of our flesh and following its desires and thoughts" (Romans 8:5). Without Christ, we are dead, deserving of wrath, following the ways of this world, and like the walkers, we shuffle along, slaves to our most basic nature.

The good news is that we are not without hope. Ephesians 2:4 begins with one of the most powerful and precious phrases in all of Scripture - "But God." Those two simple words overflow with eternal significance and hope. Humanity lay dead in its sinful state, "But God is so rich in mercy, and he loved us so much, that even though we were dead because of our sins, he gave us life when he raised Christ from the dead (Ephesians 2:4-5).

Paul contrasts our former dead way of life with the new life we've been given in Christ. We were all dead to sin, living for pleasure and gratification. *But.* But God was merciful. He didn't leave us in this state. Instead, because of His great mercy, He sent Jesus, who "made us alive together with Christ" by grace. God chose to raise us to new life, with the power to say no to our sinful nature and live the life to which we are called.

Through the grace of God, we have victory in Christ and can celebrate life over both walking and eternal death. In Ephesians 1:20-22, Paul reminded us of God's incontrovertible victory over His enemies, and he follows up in Ephesians 2:5-6 by reminding believers of the unbreakable bond between God and His people. Because Christ is seated at the right hand of His Father with all creation under His dominion, all those whose allegiance is to the King of Heaven need not fear. We can stand firm knowing that by grace, we are saved (Ephesians 2:5). We are seated with Him in the heavenly places in Christ. Remember, Ephesians 2:2 described Satan as the "prince of the power of the air." Before salvation, we dwelt in Satan's kingdom, *but God* - there's that phrase again - brought us into His kingdom, giving us a seat at His celestial "table." One day we'll celebrate the Great Banquet, the Marriage Supper of the Lamb (Revelation 19:7-10), but until then, we have a place administering and furthering that kingdom on earth.

Being raised to new life in Christ (v.6) is much more than changing our desires and behaviors. Before salvation, we are dead in sin, whereas after salvation, we are dead to sin. There is an eternity of difference between the two. Through the indwelling of the Holy Spirit, we are raised with supernatural power to resist the lies and temptation by which Satan tries to deceive and defeat us. Our salvation is more than a "fire escape out of hell." Instead, because His Spirit lives within us, we are freed to live as God designed us.

Throughout Ephesians 1, Paul reminded us that God did not leave us in our fallen state but instead chose us to be sons and daughters as co-heirs with Christ Himself. He foreordained that we would be reconciled to Himself through the death, burial, and resurrection of His Son, Jesus Christ. "For God so loved the world that he gave his one and only Son, that whoever believes in him shall not perish but have eternal life. For God did not send his Son into the world to condemn the world, but to save the world through him" (John 3:16-17).

Note that we are "seated with him in the heavenly realms because we are united with Christ Jesus" (v.6). It is not only incredible that God would elevate us to such a lofty position, it is even more staggering to consider why He would elevate us in such a way. "So God can point to us in all future ages as examples of the incredible wealth of his grace and kindness toward us, as shown in all he has done for us who are united with Christ Jesus." (v.7). All the sin that enslaved us, the wrath that should have been poured out on us, is all overpowered by God's infinite and matchless grace. His grace is infinite because He is infinite. His grace is matchless because there is none other like Him.

Ephesians 2:8-9 are two of the most significant verses in all of Scripture. Salvation is by grace through faith. That's it. There's no addendum, no caveats, no subclauses or conditions. Good works cannot save a person; it is 100% God's work in our lives. No amount of charitable giving, volunteer hours, or good intentions can secure your home in heaven. Neither can church attendance, being baptized, nor taking communion. Salvation is by grace alone.

"Grace" means that God gives us something which we do not deserve, in this case, salvation. Our sins mean we deserve judgment, but instead, God, in His infinite mercy, chooses grace, allowing us to be reconciled to Him. Go back to the analogy of a child opening a present we saw in chapter 1. That child cannot take credit for the gift in any way - a gift, by definition, is given without being earned and without expectation of reciprocation. So likewise, our salvation is provided by a sinless Father to His sinful children. We are unworthy yet made worthy in Him.

One of the most powerful events I've ever experienced as a Christian was a baptism service held at Expectation Church on Easter Sunday, 2022. Not only did we celebrate the resurrection of our Savior, but 33 people passed through the water of baptism and were "buried in the likeness of His death; raised *to walk* in newness of life" (Romans 6:4). We do not walk in our own strength nor boast in anything other than the cross - our salvation is a gift sealed by God's infinite grace. It is by this grace we are saved, and it is in this grace we walk in the good works God has prepared for us, His children.

You may say, "Well then, why bother doing good deeds?" Paul stops this line of thinking before it even starts by telling us that while they cannot save us, we have been created for this very purpose. God designed us with unique gifts and talents to do what He calls us to do in order to build His kingdom. He has given us the resources and the opportunities to do these good deeds. We are to "redeem the time" (Ephesians 5:16) because every day we allow to pass without fulfilling God's plan for us is a day utterly wasted.

Discussion Questions

1. Would you say you are thriving or just surviving? Why do you think this is the case?

2. What can we actively do to ward off the "infection" of sin?

3. What is one area of your life that God has helped you change after bringing you to Him? Share about your change in attitude toward this sin and any steps taken to help achieve victory.

4. Explain the importance of the short phrase, "But God."

5. Does "that" in verse 8 refer to the grace of God or the faith?

6. Explain the connection between verses 8-9 and 10 if good deeds cannot save us.

7. God wants us to learn from His model of generosity. As He has graciously shared with us out of His immeasurable riches, so we should generously share with others. What is one resource God has given you that you can generously share? How will you do this?

8. How would knowing that we are seated "spiritually" with the Father change your direction in life?

Chapter 4 - Welcome to the Family

Ephesians 2:11-22

In the early morning of August 13, 1961, the world changed while the people of Berlin slept. The German Democratic Republic, also known as East Germany, secretly began erecting barriers to seal off entry points from East Berlin into the western part of the city. It was a shocking turn of events that left Germans on both sides of the new border stunned.

The events that led to the construction of the Berlin Wall date back to the end of World War II. At the Yalta and Potsdam peace conferences, the Allies determined that Germany's territories would be split into four Allied Occupation Zones. The eastern part of the country was ceded to control by the Soviet Union, and the west went to the United States, Great Britain, and eventually, France. As the capital city, Berlin would be divided between the two factions.

More than 25 years later, on June 12, 1987, U.S. President Ronald Reagan stood in front of the Brandenburg Gate in Berlin and uttered his famous challenge to Mikail Gorbachev, President of the Soviet Union, "Mr. Gorbachev, tear down this wall." It took nearly three more years, but on November 9, 1989, the German people themselves finally tore down the barrier between East and West Germany, uniting both countries under one flag and one leader.

While this was clearly a momentous unifying event, there is a far more significant reunification in human history that is at the heart of Paul's letter to the Ephesians, that of God uniting Jew and Gentile within His family, tearing down the barrier that separated them.

In the Old Testament, God placed Israel at the center of the Gentile nations as a light to those outside the covenant with Abraham (Genesis 10; Genesis 12:1–3; Isaiah 42:6). He promised that unification would come when the kings of other nations would bring their riches into His kingdom and bow before Him (Isaiah 60:10–14). Implicit in His promise is that repentant Gentiles would be fellow citizens alongside Abraham's descendants. We cannot overlook the significance of this covenant because, in Paul's day, the Jews regarded the Gentiles as outsiders. Conversely, Gentiles saw the Jews as equally ignorant of God and defined by Jewish history and tradition.

The first hint of unity we see is where Paul establishes a common link between Jews and Christians in the absence of a visible deity of worship.

The word Paul uses in verse 12 to describe the Gentiles as having no god is the same word from which we derive our English word atheist. Ironically, that's what the Gentiles called the Jews and then Christians. This is because neither had statues or figures of their gods, nor, as far as the Gentiles could see, did they offer sacrifices, consult oracles and seers, or follow any of the other practices of pagans associated with worship. So Paul stands with Jewish leaders of his day and boldly declares that the Gentile's pagan gods aren't gods at all, and their followers are, in reality, worshiping a deity that doesn't exist. Instead, Paul proclaims that Jesus Christ is the promised Savior of the one, true God, placing both non-Jewish believers and Jewish people together in the same category under one God.

Paul had his work cut out for him, though, as there were many hurdles to unification. Pious Jews saw themselves as pure and undefiled because of their Jewish heritage and their observance of ceremonial laws. They viewed the Gentiles as ceremonially unclean. For example, for the Jewish people, male circumcision was—and is still today—the mark of the covenant between them and God, a physical representation that they were distinct from all other people in the world.

Yes, the Jews were God's chosen people, but Paul is saying that Gentiles are chosen as well through belief in Jesus Christ for Salvation. God did not set the Jewish people apart because of who they were, but because of who He is, which many did not understand. Most Jews in Paul's day, notably religious leaders like the

Pharisees and Sadducees, emphasized their rules and ceremonies over belief in Jesus. In fact, many rejected Him as Messiah. They failed to see that their sin was what ultimately separated them from God - their heritage was never enough to save them.

Circumcision was not the means of salvation. Nowhere in Scripture are we told that good deeds or obedience to God's law are enough to redeem us from our sin. Instead, circumcision was a physical reminder of God's covenant of grace with His people, Israel. He is their God; they are His people. No other nation can make such a claim. However, the problem lies in the notion that the Jewish perspective in Paul's time was that there are only two people groups on earth: God's people (the Jews) and everyone else (the Gentiles).

We learn in Ephesians how Paul sets out to rectify this misperception and unify God's family through Jesus Christ. Paul describes the Gentiles as "excluded from citizenship in Israel," "foreigners to the covenants of the promise," "without hope," "without God in the world," and "far away." To the Jews, the Gentiles were unclean and *utterly* separated from God with no hope of salvation. The Jews had forgotten that true circumcision was circumcision of the heart, one that led to a life of holiness and separation from the world, a life dedicated to God. Paul explains how this true circumcision was - and is - available to all people through Jesus Christ.

As a physical symbol, circumcision is similar to the physical symbol of baptism for the believer in Christ. Baptism by immersion signifies our relationship with

Christ and separation from the world. For the believer, baptism is a public profession of a personal confession. Colossians 2:13 says, "When you were dead in your sins and in the uncircumcision of your flesh, God made you alive with Christ. He forgave us all our sins."

While Gentiles could not be citizens of Israel because they were not descended from Abraham, God always intended to unify His family of believers regardless of national origin. God made a covenant of promise with Abraham and renewed it with Isaac and Jacob. God promised the Jews their own land, a priesthood, many people, and a nation. But just as circumcision demarcated the Jews as God's covenant people from the rest of the world, Jesus has made a new covenant. He brings Jews and Gentiles together under one banner, by one flesh—His own. In His body, His flesh, through His death on the cross, Jesus sets aside the old regulations and the law with its commandments.

We begin to understand how Paul intends to encourage unity through the enlightenment of equality as we read more of the book of Ephesians. Paul reasoned that both Jew and Gentile are unclean, that is, sinful and separated from a holy God. The only cleansing that would eternally purify any of them was that of salvation through Jesus Christ. Apart from Him, both Jews and Gentiles are without hope and separated from God, but through Jesus, both can be redeemed and reconciled to Him. Ephesians 2:13 is one of the most pivotal verses in Scripture. "But now in Christ Jesus, you who once were far away have been brought near by the blood of Christ." it is impossible to fully articulate the dramatic transformation between our desperate fallen state from verses 11 and 12 to verse 13.

To this point in history, Jews and Gentiles had lived separately. Jewish people considered the Gentiles outside the covenant and therefore beyond saving, while the Gentiles resented these assertions of damnation. Jesus, through Paul, reveals the sinfulness of both Jew and Gentile and offers the gift of salvation to both. Only through Jesus Christ can both be reconciled as sons and daughters of God.

This is true reconciliation, true unification.

Because of Jesus' death, we are all one (v. 14), our hostility toward others is put to death (v. 16), each of us has access to the Holy Spirit (v. 18), we are no longer strangers to God (v. 19), and are being "built" into a holy temple with Christ as the chief cornerstone (v. 20-21). Just as God chose to dwell in the Holy of Holies in the Old Testament, He now chooses to live in His church - we are his temple (Leviticus 16:2, 2 Corinthians 6:16, Hebrews 6:19-20, Hebrews 8:7-13, Hebrews 9:11-12). Our salvation is so much more than merely the forgiveness of sin. Instead, it is the integration into God's work of redemption and reconciliation (2 Corinthians 5).

Only when we read the old covenant through the lens of Jesus and His new covenant can we truly understand the intended unification of God's family through reconciliation of Jews and Gentiles. Jesus, God incarnate, took on human form and dwelt among us. In John 1:14, the phrase "He dwelt among us" in some translations is more literally translated as "He tabernacled among us," or "He pitched a tent among us." The Old Testament tabernacle was where God lived and moved among his people. God established His tabernacle in the wilderness to foreshadow the true tabernacle which was to come, Jesus, the Messiah. "For in Him, all the fullness of Deity dwells in bodily form" (Colossians. 2:9). Jesus is the lens through which we must read the Old Testament; otherwise, those 39 books are little more than historical record. Only when we read it in light of Jesus' incarnation, life, death, and resurrection can we understand it fully and appreciate the reconciliation between Jew and Gentile. Through faith in Him, we are gathered into the body of Christ, which is the temple of the Holy Spirit (Ephesians 2:19-22; 1 Corinthians 3:16-17).

Paul's temple analogy would have resonated with Jewish believers. He turned one of the central symbols of Judaism on end because the temple was the heart of their faith. It was where heaven and earth met and where the nation came together at the seat of political, social, and cultural life. By using the tabernacle as his illustration, Paul not only made his point but spoke directly to the heart of the people.

The Gentiles would also have understood the meaning of Paul's temple analogy. Remember, Ephesus was the seat of the cult of Artemis. Ancient historian, Pliny the Elder, described her temple in the heart of the city as "the most wonderful monument of Græcian magnificence." Just as the tabernacle in the wilderness was the heart of Jewish faith, commerce, and society, so too was the Temple of Artemis for the Gentiles. By using an illustration that spoke to both

Jew and Gentile, Paul's analogy mirrors God's plan of reunification for both peoples.

We cannot understand God's plan of salvation for all humanity apart from the scarlet thread of Jesus Christ that runs through Scripture. From eternity past, God planned to redeem humanity through the people of Israel, the Jews. Scripture carefully records Israel as witnesses to God's creational intent for this world. They had a front-row seat to the promises of God to restore and redeem. They are the ones through whom God would accomplish both. Despite their struggles and failures, the history of the Jewish people is seamlessly interwoven with the story of God's redemptive plan for humanity. Through them, we see God's faithfulness to complete the mission of redemption and to do it using the nation of Israel.

Jesus brought peace and reconciliation through His redemptive work on the cross, unifying believers under Him into a universal, spiritual temple made of consecrated people. There is one Christ, one sacrifice, and one temple. All are independent of man's rules and laws.

While Adam's sin brought the curse of death, Jesus' death cancels that curse; though Adam's disobedience makes us all sinners, Jesus' obedience means all, Jew and Gentile alike, will be accounted "righteous," as Christ's perfect righteousness is imputed to us through faith.

Once cast from the garden, hiding from the shame of disobedience and pride, condemned by sin and shame, we are now privileged to walk humbly with God in perfect fellowship now and in the garden to come.

Discussion Questions

1. Since they were outside God's covenant, could Gentiles in the Old Testament be saved? How?

2. Why is it important that a church celebrate diversity within its unity? How does the gospel allow us to do this?

3. Consider how those receiving this letter might have reacted. How easy or difficult do you think it was for them to live out the oneness they were called to as followers of Christ?

4. Paul describes our equality in Jesus with three images: citizens, a family, and a building. How is each of these words descriptive of people before and after they become Christians?

5. If Paul were speaking to you or your congregation about reconciliation, would his words be ones of praise or disappointment?

6. Consider the magnitude of being cast from the garden and condemned to now experiencing the privilege of intimate fellowship with God. How does that impact how you value your salvation?

Chapter 5 - God's Mystery Revealed

Ephesians 3:1-13

One summer vacation in elementary school, I found a battered copy of Agatha Christie's *And Then There Were None* on my grandfather's bookshelf. I read it in a single afternoon, swaying in a hammock, mesmerized by the story. To this day, a good mystery is still my favorite way to while away an afternoon. I love the slow build of suspense, the red herrings that are woven into the story, and the denouement, that "Aha!" moment that makes you gasp and say, "I knew it!" or, even better, "What? Of course, the butler did it!"

Clearly, I'm not the only one intrigued by a mystery. The internet has given rise to a horde of armchair detectives who spend hours in chat rooms, private Facebook groups, and the Twitterverse, postulating on the truth behind who and where D.B. Cooper is, or the fate of the crew of the Mary Celeste, or searching for the identity of Jack the Ripper. Mysteries have captivated our collective conscience that streaming services have entire categories dedicated to true crime, mysteries, and cases that have fascinated generations.

So it is natural that when we read the term "mystery" in Ephesians 3 to assume Paul is referring to something that must be investigated because it remains unsolved. Yet, he's not referring to an Agatha Christie-style thriller or a cold case. Instead, he speaks of a three-part mystery more complex than we can comprehend. The "mystery" Paul speaks of is not something to be solved or uncovered, but rather, that which was previously unknown has now been revealed. "This mystery is that the Gentiles are fellow heirs, members of the same body, and partakers of the promise in Christ Jesus through the gospel" (Ephesians 3:6).

At the time he was writing his letter to the Ephesians, Paul was under house arrest in Rome for preaching Christ. Religious leaders opposed his teaching and pressured the Roman authorities to arrest him and bring him to trial for treason and inciting rebellion among the Jews. Paul had appealed his case to be heard by the emperor and was awaiting the emperor's response (Acts 28:16-31). Paul never wavered in his belief that God was in control of his circumstances and had a plan for his life.

Paul says that he is "the prisoner of Christ Jesus" and considers his situation inclusive of his ministry. He does not consider himself a prisoner of the Roman Empire, local authorities, or the Jewish leaders who pressed for his arrest. Instead, Paul says he is a prisoner of Christ for the sake of the Gentiles. There is no accusation or condemnation in his words. Instead, Paul's deep love for his Messiah has given him a commitment to following the mission of Christ which presses him to preach and reach the Gentiles. Paul isn't looking for sympathy; on the contrary, He counts it a joy to be imprisoned for Jesus. Paul will reiterate these sentiments later in verse 13.

From eternity past, God's mysteries all revolve around His glorious inclusive plan. He had a plan for Paul's life, for you and me, and for all of humanity, unfolding from the Garden of Eden through eternity. That plan includes this mystery, that of God reconciling Gentiles to Himself. Paul references his part in this plan given to him by God in a revelation: preach the gospel to the Gentiles. Here in the opening verses of Ephesians 3, he uses the revelation of the mystery to challenge the Ephesians to stay strong in their faith despite his imprisonment and uses the church's identity in Christ as a template for daily Christian living.

God reveals His plans in His perfect timing, which can in itself prove to be a mystery to us. He hadn't kept His plan for reconciliation a secret because He wanted to deceive or hide something from His people, but because He intended it to be revealed at the perfect time. The Jewish people who lived during the time of the Old Testament knew that the Gentiles would someday receive salvation (Isaiah 49:6), but what wasn't revealed was that all Jewish and Gentile believers would be equal in God's family. Jesus broke down those barriers when He broke down the "wall of hostility" and created one new people (Ephesians 2: 14-15).

This inclusion over hostile barriers was essential to God's plan for a path to righteousness. Prior to Jesus' sacrificial death on the cross, salvation was found only in the Levitical administration of God's grace. God didn't have to provide a path to righteousness, atonement for our sins, or enter into a covenant with His people, but He demonstrated His grace through the Law. But what about the Gentiles? Were they condemned to eternal damnation because they weren't God's chosen people, without the Law and outside the covenant? That was not God's plan at all.

In Paul's letter to the Ephesians, we begin to realize that God never intended to save one nation over or at the expense of another, but quite possibly the opposite. One might argue there is a secret plan of inclusion at play. We once knew the Jewish way to reconciliation with a Jewish God, one that would be brought by a Jewish Messiah to the Jews. Now we learn that the one way to reconciliation with the one true God has come from God's chosen people, brought by the one true Messiah, to Jew and Gentile alike.

We may be tempted to view the Law of the Old Testament as works-based salvation without any measure of grace. However, that school of thought is deeply flawed because the Law itself was given in God's abundant grace. He did not offer it to all mankind but to a chosen people, the Jews, which is also an act of grace. However, the Law was quickly exposed as insufficient, not from a deficiency on God's part, but because His act of grace exposed man's deficiency to exist in covenant with God. Even though the Jews were chosen by God, given a covenantal pathway to atonement, and provided explicit instructions about how they could live in a relationship with God, they failed to do so.

In the mystery made known through Christ, God did not abolish the Law but fulfilled it on our behalf through Christ. He did this for all humanity, so the covenantal relationship is now experienced through faith, not temple sacrifice. God's grace has found its fullest expression in Christ, and the Law has exposed the reality that we are entirely dependent upon this grace. Furthermore, God's grace is made fuller in that He has reconciled the Jew and the Gentile under the administration of His grace in Christ.

The mystery of His all-inclusive grace is what Paul was made to realize by God's revelation to him. Paul is on a mission to bring this good news to the Ephesians and beyond to all Gentiles. He wants the world to know the good news of God's grace in the finished work of Jesus Christ. Because of Jesus, all who would believe in Him in faith can live in a covenantal relationship with God.

What are the terms of this new covenant? Simply that He is our God, and we, His people. This is why Paul says that "in Him and through faith we may approach God with freedom and confidence" (v. 11). It is because of Jesus that we can, in faith, approach God freely, knowing that we are accepted; not because we adhere to the Law and righteousness, but because of Jesus!

Throughout his ministry, Paul drew not only on the power of the gospel but the tools his education and life experience provided to communicate the good news. This, too, was all part of God's divine, inclusive plan. Paul, a Pharisee, was once deeply and profoundly proud of his Jewish heritage. He was one of God's chosen people, living with the inherent favor of God. To be convinced that the dividing line between Jew and Gentile has been eliminated and that through the gospel, the Gentiles are heirs together with Israel, members together of one body, and sharers together in the promise of Christ Jesus is a monumental shift in Paul's mindset. It demonstrates a complete conversion that is further shown in Paul's mission.

For a Phariseelike Paul to go to the Gentiles with the good news of the gospel and usher them into the one family of God is remarkable. When he refers to himself as the least deserving of God's people, Paul recognizes that despite his education, his standing and privilege as a Roman citizen, and his passion for preaching the gospel, none of it would be possible without God's help. Despite his past as a persecutor of the church, God chose *Paul* to be His missionary to the Gentiles and fully equipped him to complete that mission.

So what does all this mean for us today? Simply this: God's secret plan is that the death and resurrection of Christ allows all people - Jew and Gentile alike - to enter equally into God's promises.

This mystery that has been revealed is not just for the chosen few but is fulfilled and manifested in the Church.

Communities that are outcasts, oppressed, or considered "other" have perfect equality in God's kingdom. Within the Church, individuals from every background have been united into one family, regardless of how our culture regards them. This is the kind of love we need to show to one another no matter who they are.

God's plan is that the Church be a living witness to the power of the gospel, reconciling individuals to God and one another. Christianity has no place for prejudice, bigotry, racism, or hatred toward others because God Himself has no favorites. We are all image-bearers of God, and His mercy and compassion are extended to all. Every one of us, without exception, is oppressed by sin, unable to redeem ourselves through good works, but the gift of salvation is available to all through the work of Jesus Christ on the cross.

That is the good news of the gospel that is available to all. That is the mystery revealed; we who were once exiled from the garden are welcomed home into the family of God. We have an inheritance, are included as part of God's family, and become joint heirs with Jesus with full access to our heavenly Father, who has a plan and a purpose for even, as Paul said of himself, the least of us. While we view him through the lens of history as one of the great heroes of faith, Paul says that he doesn't deserve to proclaim this gospel, but God is graciously using him to proclaim His grace to the Gentiles. God shows Paul grace and then offers grace to others through Paul. The mystery is revealed through Paul (and others) to all the peoples of the world (Jews and Gentiles) because of the grace of God! Now, all people have access to the "incalculable riches of Christ."

St. Augustine said, "In the Old Testament, the New Testament is concealed; in the New Testament, the Old Testament is revealed." God's plan for humanity is the scarlet thread of Jesus' sacrificial gift of salvation, woven throughout eternity, tying the Old and the New Testaments together. Everything God plans to reveal in the New Testament is seeded and planted in the Old. As Malachi closes the Old Testament, we anticipate those seeds blossoming into fulfilled prophecies. In the New Testament, they bloom and grow in the light of God's redemptive plan, creating a new and beautiful garden.

From the despair of Adam and Eve's expulsion from the Garden of Eden, God demonstrates His infinite mercy, grace, and love for us in this new garden of revelation.

Discussion Questions

1. Paul relates the mystery to the gospel by calling it the "mystery of Christ." In Ephesians 3:5, he offers unique insights into this mystery. What are those insights? Why is this important in helping the Church understand the nature of Paul's imprisonment?

2. Does knowing this mystery change how you should read and understand the Old Testament?

3. What part does this mystery play in terms of racial reconciliation?

4. What could we do more in our church to show we want racial and social barriers removed?

5. Gentiles and Jews are considered equal under salvation. What challenges do we face among other races in sharing our faith? What approaches must we have?

6. Paul was a powerful preacher and evangelist who used his education, testimony, and imprisonment to present the gospel. Consider your life story. How does God want to use you? What part of your story can be used as a tool to share with the lost?

7. The heart of Ephesians 3:1-13 is verse 10, one of the New Testament's most powerful statements about the existence of the church. How can we, as a community of faith, explore the riches of Christ as described by Paul?

Chapter 6 - Power and Love

Ephesians 3:14-22

That great poet of our age, Meatloaf, once said, "I would do anything for love, but I won't do that." Where does the man who once picked up a hitchhiking Charles Manson and who proposed to his wife, not with a diamond ring, but with a dead salmon, draw the line? I, for one, don't want to know.

The power of love and the love of power have shaped the course of human history. It is the theme of countless films, artwork, and literature. It has led weak men to do powerful things, and powerful men to act carelessly with no regard for consequences. In fact, it sometimes seems the more rich and powerful the individual, the more reckless the behavior. Look no further than Paris, Prince of Troy, and his lover, Helen, known to history as "the face that launched a thousand ships." Their actions kicked off the ten-year conflict known as the Trojan War.

The Trojan War was the start of the Bronze Age conflict between the kingdoms of Troy and Mycenaean Greece that blurs the lines of history and mythology. Helen was betrothed to the king of Sparta, Menelaus, but secretly in a relationship with Paris. Things escalated when Paris kidnapped Helen on her wedding night, escaping with her to Troy. Unsurprisingly, Menelaus was furious and convinced his brother Agamemnon, king of Mycenae, to lead an expedition to retrieve her. Agamemnon's forces were accompanied by a fleet of more than a thousand ships to lay siege to Troy and demand Helen's return.

What began as a rescue mission dragged into a ten-year siege of the city. According to legend - with a little mythology tossed in for flavor, these are the ancient Greeks we're talking about after all - a lord named Odysseus came up with a brilliant plan to resolve the conflict. He and fifty of his men hid inside a colossal wooden horse that the Greeks offered as a gift to the Trojans as they pretended to retreat from their camp. After much debate, the Trojans eventually opened the gates and brought the statue inside the city. Later that night, Odysseus and his men snuck out of the horse, re-opened the gates of Troy, and signaled to the Greek warships concealed just offshore to invade. The Trojans were massacred, and the city was ransacked and almost destroyed. Menelaus then sailed home with Helen, who ruled at his side until his death. Some sources say Helen was exiled to the island of Rhodes, where a vengeful war widow had her hanged.

Power and love are the forces that shaped the ancient world and continue to drive and shape our world today. They are also the two central themes of Paul's prayer for young believers. It is both his focus in the latter half of Ephesians 3 and serves as the capstone or exclamation point to the first three chapters. Clearly, this focus indicates it is a pivotal point in Paul's letter.

After two and a half chapters of doctrine, Paul is about to dive deeply into three chapters of application and imperatives. In his words we can see the awe Paul feels in the majesty of the gospel. God the Father so loved us that He had a plan for our redemption from eternity past, rescuing us from sin and damnation, adopting us as sons and daughters, and placing us in the Church, a living body, for all the world to see. But Paul's prayer also reflects our deep need to surrender so that God can work in our hearts if we are to become true disciples. These few verses are among the most powerful in Scripture. If you've ever felt inadequate or unable to live the life Christ has called you to, this prayer is for you. If you've ever felt unworthy, unloveable, or too far gone, let these words sink into your heart so you can know how deeply you are loved and be reminded you are chosen.

There is nothing casual or superficial about Paul's prayer. It is clear here and elsewhere in his writings that Paul was dependent in prayer—not just on prayer—and recognized that he could never achieve what God called him to do unless God worked in and through him. Paul understood that prayer is our channel to connect to God's power, express our dependence on Him, and access divine wisdom and leadership. Prayer is the heartbeat of Paul's ministry and the source of God's extraordinary anointing of his preaching, teaching, and writing.

Paul wants these young believers in Ephesus to see that prayer brings together love and power. He wants them to understand the love that grows between God and the individual as they pray and the supernatural power of God that flows from God to and through that person. He prays that God would strengthen their "inner being" (v. 16). The goal is not physical strength, but spiritual strength. Remember, Paul was imprisoned in Rome as he was writing this epistle. He would not have been the only one to face opposition for the gospel's sake. His followers would have faced a level of persecution as well. Ephesus was a pagan city, and the merchants and city's elite would have been eager to suppress any further spread of Paul's teaching.

The phrase "so that Christ may dwell in your hearts through faith" (v. 17) is not one to be overlooked. Though we each receive the indwelling of the Holy Spirit upon accepting Christ, Paul wants more than the Holy Spirit's presence in our lives—he wants us to allow the Holy Spirit to lead and influence every area of our lives. This ties closely with Ephesians 2, where Paul reminds us that Christ has made us citizens and fellow heirs with full reign in the Kingdom of God, not as strangers but as sons and daughters. Just as we are given to reign in our Father's Kingdom, Christ must be given free reign over our innermost being. In a demonstration of our love for the Father, we should, as His followers, submit to His authority over us.

Paul continues his prayer by emphasizing "being rooted and grounded in love." Psalm 1 explains this rooting and grounding perfectly:

> "Oh, the joys of those who do not follow the advice of the wicked, or stand around with sinners, or join in with mockers. But they delight in the law of the Lord, meditating on it day and night. They are like trees planted along the riverbank, bearing fruit each season. Their leaves never wither, and they prosper in all they do."

Like the tree whose roots run deep, keeping it safe through drought and storm, God's love secures and establishes the believer.

The world has taken the concept of love and twisted it to the place where its meaning and value are far from what Paul longs for believers to experience. We love pizza. We love to travel. We love a particular movie, sport, or athlete. Even the love between a husband and wife falls short. Our understanding of love is finite and sometimes selfish. "I'll love you if you love me," or I'll love you as long as you do what makes me happy." That's the kind of love that causes conflict in relationships and is far from the love Christ has demonstrated for us. His love is unchanging and everlasting. The Greek word Paul uses for knowledge, *katalabesthai*, encompasses experience, not just head knowledge. The only way we can understand God's love is to experience it personally.

Paul's prayer also suggests that believers would be filled with the fullness of God. This concept of fullness is reflected in Psalm 42:1-2. "As a deer pants for flowing streams, so pants my soul for you, O God. My soul thirsts for God, for the living God." We should desire to be filled with the fullness of God because, when we are filled with Him, the distractions of this world become less important. We think more like God thinks as we attain more and more the mind of Christ.

Finally, Paul's passion in prayer reaches a crescendo in the last verses of chapter three. Considering the glory of God, Paul can't help praising God for His goodness to His children. We serve a God who does things for us from which we have never thought to pray or ask for protection. The Psalmist, referring to the Most High God, says, "For he will command his angels concerning you to guard you in all your ways" (Psalm 91:11). Though angels are all around us, it is not a guardian angel that keeps you from harm, it is God himself. This distinction is important. God commissions angels to watch over and protect believers at His command. They are not independent beings but are under His authority and instruction. In fact, we know angels themselves are curious about the salvation God offers humans and how He chooses to work through His people. In 1 Corinthians 4:9, Paul describes the apostles as a "spectacle" not only for people but also for the angels. God alone leads, guides, directs, and protects in ways far beyond what we could comprehend.

Furthermore, as we pray for each other, we begin to experience God working in ways we haven't asked for or imagined. Scripture contains many examples of individuals who couldn't have dreamed all God would do in their lives.

Abram did not expect to become Abraham, the Father of many nations (Genesis 11-26).

Moses never envisioned leaving the palace so he could lead the Children of Israel out of bondage in Egypt toward the Promised Land (Exodus 1-12).

Noah could not have anticipated a global flood that would wipe out all but his family and the animals he placed on the ark (Genesis 5-9).

Esther had no way of knowing that her faith in God and courage to stand before the king would save her people from genocide (Esther 1-10).

Mary had no idea that she'd be chosen to bear the Son of God in the flesh or that Joseph would stand by her while the world whispered about her miraculous pregnancy (Luke 1-2).

Neither the unnamed Samaritan woman knew she would meet the Messiah at midday as she drew water, nor could Zacchaeus have known he'd be summoned from his perch in a tree to host the Savior in his home (John 4:1-42; Luke 19:1-8).

No one understood these experiences better than Saul, who couldn't have anticipated his encounter with God on the road to Damascus that would transform him from Saul the persecutor to Paul the Apostle (Acts 9:1-30).

None of these individuals was loved or chosen by God in greater measure than He loves or chooses us. Yet, they did have one thing in common—God granted them faith. How did they nurture such faith? From spending time in prayer, drawing close to God, seeing His hand at work, and falling ever deeper in love with Him. Likewise, as we grow in our faith, we too will experience unimaginable things in Him.

As you pray, pray in faith, knowing that God desires to be in communion with His children. Paul reminds us later in Philippians 4:19 that "God will meet all your needs according to the riches of his glory in Christ Jesus." So, though we may not always get what we want, rest in contentment knowing you have all you need. Such is the power and love of our heavenly Father.

Discussion Questions

1. We are dependent in prayer just as Jesus was (Luke 5:16; Luke 6:12-16). What's the difference between being dependent in prayer versus dependent on prayer?

2. Why is the statement, "All we can do now is pray," contrary to what Scripture teaches about prayer?

3. What are some of God's "glorious riches" that might be helpful in our lives?

4. Scripture tells us that if we are properly rooted, properly constructed on a foundation of Christ's love, nothing can shake us. What does that look like in our day-to-day life? What does it look like when trials and heartbreak inevitably come our way?

5. What are some examples of the height of God's love? Depth? Length? Width? Read these passages for more ideas: Psalm 103:11-12, Micah 7:19, Jeremiah 31:3, John 3:16; Revelation 13:8

Chapter 7 - Christian Maturity

Ephesians 4:1-16

Someone once said, "Maturity is not measured by age. It is an attitude built by experience." Babies become toddlers, who become preschoolers, then children, tweens, teens, adults, and on through the stages of adulthood. Theoretically, our experiences shape us, and hopefully, we learn lessons that equip us for the challenges life throws our way.

In reality, life doesn't always follow this path of maturity. For instance, we all know children and teenagers who demonstrate maturity and wisdom far beyond their years. They have faced grief and loss, have been food insecure, or lived in unstable, sometimes violent homes, and their exposure to the ugly side of life has forced them to age into tiny adults. On the other hand, we know adults who seem to have skated through life with parents who snowplowed their path, enabling them to dodge every obstacle, leaving them as fragile as a snowflake and incapable of "adulting."

Compare the maturity levels of the average American fourth grader against a child living in a country ripped apart by war or devastated by famine. One is blessed to go to school and has ready access to food, clean drinking water, and a safe place to sleep at night. The other lives in constant fear and often goes to bed hungry, dirty, and unsure of what the next day will hold. There are miles and miles of distance between their maturity levels.

Likewise, just because someone has grown up in church or professed Christ at an early age does not mean they are spiritually mature. God has made you alive with Christ (Ephesians 2:4); that's our new birth through salvation. A Christian isn't born into adulthood. We are born into infancy and then must strive toward spiritual maturity.

In chapter four of his letter to the Ephesians, Paul wants us to understand that our spiritual maturity impacts our practical living. In other words, our spiritual maturity determines how we live out the mission to which God has called us. Our relationship with Christ influences all other relationships, both within the Church and out in the community.

Paul moves on to explain the responsibilities of believers now that he has established the necessary foundation of salvation in Christ. Since God has done so much work to bring unity to His people, so should His people join Him in sustaining such harmony. Therefore, we must "make every effort to keep the unity of the Spirit through the bond of peace" (Ephesians 4:3). This behavior will demonstrate a mature understanding of God's redemptive love and salvation.

Paul tells the Ephesian believers that full maturity is God's goal for the Christian and the Church. He gives them three measures by which they can determine their individual and congregational maturity: unity, ministry, and discernment.

In verses 1-6, Paul discusses what it means to be unified in Christ through the Holy Spirit. He urges them to walk in a manner worthy of the gospel by walking in humility, gentleness, patience, and forbearing love. Collectively, these lead to unity. That's why he challenges us to "be eager to maintain the unity of the Spirit in the bond of peace." This unity isn't something we can manufacture through determination. On the contrary, unity is produced by the Holy Spirit. Spiritual maturity may be difficult to define, but it is easy to spot - it looks like dependence on the Holy Spirit. We model humility, gentleness, patience, and long-suffering love leading to peace in all of our relationships. Living and serving in unity is amark of the mature believer.

Unity is exemplified in the Holy Trinity. It is important to note here that verses 4-6 are a trinitarian passage of Scripture. It is true that there truly is only one Lord (Jesus) and only one faith (in Jesus), and one baptism (in the name of Jesus) (v.5). Furthermore, there is only one God who is the Father of all and is over all, and through all, and in all (v. 6). There is also only one body and one Spirit (v. 4). This Holy Spirit ensures the hope of our calling in Jesus Christ (Ephesians 1:13-14). It is in the One Spirit, One Lord, and One God (Spirit, Son, and Father) that our unity is to be based. This only makes sense if the Three are One. This unity is our model for the unity we are called to within the church.

As the Holy Trinity is an example of the inexplicable unification of unique and separate parts. This unity is equipped with diversity. Paul teaches us that Christ has allocated gifts to this body of people, specifically apostles, prophets, evangelists, pastors, and teachers (v.11). God gives these gifts with a purpose: to equip this one body, this one people, which is the Church, for works of service. It is to enable the body of Christ to be built up with the vision of being in complete and total unity in the faith and the knowledge of the Son of God.

So again, God (Father, Son, and Holy Spirit) has done the work to bring about unity for His called people. He has done the work of the cross. He has put down the deposit, and He has given gifts to His children so they may be built up into the unity He has done the work to create.

We, His people, however, are not without responsibility and response in God's work. Paul tells us we are to "be completely humble and gentle, be patient and to bear with one another in love "(v. 2). We should make every effort to keep the unity of the Spirit through the bond of peace we have in Jesus (v. 4). We are to do the works of service, and we are to speak the truth in love (v. 15).

Additionally, Paul says, "Grace was given to each one of us according to the measure of Christ's gift." Each one of us, without exception, has been given spiritual gifts that Jesus wants us to use to strengthen His body, the Church. Paul lists some but not all of those gifts in v. 11 and elsewhere in his writings (Romans 12:3-8; 1 Corinthians 12:1-31; 1 Peter 4:10-11). A spiritually mature church is comprised of people who are prayerfully and actively using their abilities, resources, and inclinations to meet the needs of the body and the community around them.

Pastors are often challenged that their message isn't "going deep enough," that mature believers within the congregation aren't "being fed," or that they focus too much on the lost or new believers. Perhaps the criticism is valid. There are also those who stand on platforms every weekend, all around the world, preaching a gospel of social change rather than Biblical salvation. However, often, the issue isn't what's being offered but the spiritual maturity of the individual raising a complaint, and they mask their criticism as "speaking the truth in love."

Speaking the truth in love is one of the most challenging aspects of spiritual maturity, and the ability to do so with compassion and understanding is a gift. Unfortunately, there are some who weaponize their opinions and mask them with "speaking the truth in love." In a post-truth culture that encourages us to "speak our own truth," speaking the truth in love can be challenging. Even among fellow Christ-followers, it can be received as judgmental or insensitive. As a result, we may find ourselves speaking lies instead of truth or placing feelings over facts. It can lead us to appeal to emotions rather than intellect, and worse yet, to being friends of the world rather than friends of Christ.

To speak the truth in love takes maturity. It is speaking that which is doctrinally sound and comes from a heart committed to someone who needs correction. It is done in love for the benefit of someone who needs an adjustment to his or her attitudes or actions, not from a self-righteous place of "I know better than you." It is also imperative that it is done with the spiritual well-being of the other person in mind, not so you can tell them what you see them doing wrong. Before you open your mouth, take it to the Lord in prayer. Paul cautions us in Philippians 2:3, "Do nothing out of selfish ambition or vain conceit. Rather, in humility, value others above yourselves." This isn't about you - it is about drawing someone who has strayed back into communion with Jesus. When done from a place of compassion, not judgment, Paul tells us in 2 Timothy 2:25-26 that we can lead them to repentance. A loving, prayer-based approach helps the individual see how his or her actions create a risk of greater spiritual warfare. For every truth in Scripture, the devil has an alluring lie to deceive us.

This leads us to the third mark of spiritual maturity: discernment. To speak the truth, one must first know it. Followers of Christ must seek out sound Biblical instruction. The leaders of the Church must teach faithfully "so that we may no longer be children, tossed to and fro by the waves and carried about by every wind of doctrine, by human cunning, by craftiness in deceitful schemes" (v. 14). Paul cautioned us in 2 Timothy 4:3-4, "For a time is coming when people will no longer listen to sound and wholesome teaching. They will follow their own desires and will look for teachers who will tell them whatever their itching ears want to hear. They will reject the truth and chase after myths." Sound familiar?

Discerning truth from lies and falsehoods is a critical component of spiritual maturity. Paul tells us that Christ Himself gave us apostles, prophets, evangelists, pastors, and teachers to equip his people for works of service. Leaders were raised up "so that the body of Christ may be built up...and become mature, attaining to the whole measure of the fullness of Christ." Our spiritual growth, however, is not the sole responsibility of the pastor who stands in the pulpit, behind the podium, or paces the platform on Sunday morning. God has given us immeasurable resources so that we can study and learn to become more like Christ. As the "body of Christ" is built up, we all reach unity in the faith and become mature. It is important to use discernment before criticizing spiritual leaders. Is it possible that we examine and evaluate a church's quality by how we are maturing? That we put our own personal growth over that of the Church?

To anyone struggling with this, I would ask the following questions. Consider it a challenge for and toward unity, the fullness of Christ, and the Church as it is supposed to be:

- Have you been completely humble and gentle? Or have you been critical, suggesting you know more and know better than others in the church (including leadership)?

- Have you sincerely tried to keep the unity of the Spirit through the bond of peace? Or, instead, have you kept your feelings to yourself rather than working them out with someone you have conflict with? Have you gossiped? Have you spoken ill of others?

- Have you been patient? Or do you demand satisfaction, resolution, and discipline immediately?

- Do you expect people in the church to live up to a particular standard regardless of where they are in their faith in Christ?

- Have you been bearing with one another in love, or are you critical of every mistake you see, whether real or perceived? Are you patient in allowing others to mature and grow in their faith, or does change have to be instantaneous?

- Are you fully engaged in works of service? For example, are you an armchair quarterback or keyboard warrior with plenty to say yet little to do?

- Finally, are you speaking the truth in love? Are you confronting those things that cause conflict and disunity, or are you critical and hoping for failure so you can be proved right and say, "I told you so?"

An easy self-test for your willingness to pursue spiritual maturity is to ask yourself one simple question: Is my commitment to change or to admit I am wrong greater than my commitment to my reputation? In other words, is it more important to me to follow God's leading, or does the opinion of those around me outweigh the importance of how God sees me?

When we respond to God's work of unity, as we ought, in humility, gentleness, patience, bearing with one another in love, making every effort to keep the unity, active in works of service, and speaking the truth in love, only then will we grow and mature into what the church was always meant to be, the fullness of Christ.

As believers, God calls us to leave behind our spiritual infancy, become mature, and attain the whole measure of the fullness of Christ, for that is what the church is to be (Ephesians 1:22-23). Once this maturity and unity are realized, then we are no longer infants on turbulent waves of the sea being tossed this way and that by "every wind of doctrine" (Ephesians 4:14). Just as life experience teaches us that wise choices are necessary for survival, spiritual maturity teaches us that discernment is an essential element of our spiritual growth. Unless we study the Word, spend time in prayer, and strive to know the mind of Christ, we are easy prey for the devil who will whisper lies in our ears, leading us down a path of certain destruction.

Discussion Questions

1. Why is speaking the truth in love so difficult?

2. Have you ever been rescued from a messy situation or risky behavior by someone who chose to speak the truth in love? Conversely, can you share a time when a fellow believer disguised their venom with Scripture? What was your response?

3. What "works of service" does God call us to aid in our spiritual maturity? What does that look like as you serve in your church?

4. How are you using the gifts God has given you to contribute to the life and health of your church?

5. In Ephesians 4:7, Paul quotes Psalm 68:18, connecting the giving of gifts to Christ's ascension. What is the significance of the ascension in empowering us as the Church to fulfill the mission of the Great Commission (Matthew 28:18-20)?

6. What are your spiritual gifts? How do you demonstrate spiritual maturity using God's gifts to serve others?

Chapter 8 - True Transformation

Ephesians 4:17-32

There's no shortage of problematic reality TV shows, but in the history of the genre, it is difficult to find one more reprehensible than the FOX series "The Swan." The premise was simple—so-called "ugly ducklings" were transformed into "swans" and given a chance to compete with other "swans" in a beauty pageant. Each week for a 12-week series, audiences watched as two women underwent plastic surgery, extreme dieting, cosmetic dentistry, tough-love physical training, and two one-hour therapy sessions.

In the pilot, we meet two women, Kelly and Rachel, whose backstories are told through the "confessional" style that is the cornerstone of reality TV. The exploitation of these women with low self-esteem from years of bullying and body dysmorphia is disturbing. The physical and emotional trauma they experience is hard to watch, making you question the integrity of the professionals employed by the network. Over the three months of her transformation, Kelly undergoes cosmetic dentistry, including bleaching and veneers, a nose job, lip enhancement, a chin implant, a brow lift, liposuction on her cheeks and chin, and mastopexy. Additionally, she undergoes liposuction on her stomach, inner and outer thighs, back, and her "flanks"—the area on the sides and back of your abdomen between your lower ribs and your hips.

Meanwhile, Kelly spends two hours a day in the gym doing cardio and strength training while subsisting on 1200 calories a day—the caloric intake recommended for toddlers—to lose 39 pounds over 12 weeks. Did I mention that during those three months, Kelly is isolated from friends and family and not allowed to look in a mirror? If this sounds more like an episode of "The Twilight Zone" than a show marketed as TV14 and drawing 9.1 million viewers weekly, you're not alone in thinking so. Fortunately, slipping ratings and backlash over how the women were treated meant the show only lasted two seasons.

Humanity has been obsessed with outward appearances seemingly since time began. Archeologists have found evidence of the oldest known use of cosmetics at a dig site in the Balkans dating to a time between 4350 and 4100 BC. The findings are the oldest known evidence of cosmetic use in Europe, even older than cosmetics dated in Mesopotamia and Egypt.

But, as anyone with an ounce of common sense or life experience can tell you, appearances can be deceiving. Transforming the body doesn't translate to transforming the mind or spirit. Unfortunately, these women couldn't fix their low self-esteem with a nose job—just Google "The Swan - where are they now?" and see how damaging the show was to contestants.

True transformation only comes through renewing our minds through the Holy Spirit. Paul tells us in 1 Corinthians 5:17 that anyone who belongs to Christ has become a new person. The old life is gone; a new life has begun. Here in the second half of Ephesians chapter four, Paul dives deeper into how we are to live as followers of Christ. Just as his message in the first verses was clear about how we can have unity and grow in Christian maturity, so is his instruction on how we are to live out our testimony before unbelievers.

Transformation requires becoming a follower of Christ and living in Christ. Beginning in verse 17, Paul tells the Ephesians that they must "no longer live as the Gentiles do." When we read "Gentiles," we understand it refers to non-Jewish people. But Paul has spent the first three chapters of Ephesians explaining how God has unified Jews and Gentiles, and now God's chosen people are those in Christ. As such, Paul has effectively expanded the meaning of Gentile here in this passage to include all non-Christ followers regardless of whether they are Jew or Gentile. Previously there were God's chosen people, the Jews, and those outside of such election, the Gentiles. Now, there are God's chosen people, those in

Christ, and those outside of such election, which Paul also refers to here as the Gentiles.

Paul uses the analogy of light and darkness to illustrate the spiritual ignorance of those apart from Christ and not living in Him. When we read, "no longer live as the Gentiles do," we understand that Paul is reminding us that now that we are in Christ, there should be new behaviors that set us apart, demarcating the change Christ has brought about. It is the same verbiage he used when he stood before King Agrippa (Acts 26) and defended his mission to the Gentiles: "'... open their eyes and turn them from darkness to light, and from the power of Satan to God, so that they may receive forgiveness of sins and a place among those who are sanctified by faith in [Jesus].'" Paul understood that without awareness or sensitivity towards Christ and God's will, all sense of direction is lost. Theologian Samuel Chadwick once said, "Confusion and impotence are the inevitable results when the wisdom and resources of the world are substituted for the presence and power of the Spirit."

In Ephesians 2:11-22, Paul explained that we were alienated from Christ and His people, excluded from the promised covenants, hopeless, and without God in the world. In Ephesians 4, Paul shows us that this alienation goes even deeper. Our hopelessly confused minds keep us chasing after temporal things; money, power, sex, always hungry for more. The prophet Isaiah described this state perfectly in Isaiah 56:3. "We all, like sheep, have gone astray, each of us has turned to our own way; and the Lord has laid on him the iniquity of us all."

This corrupt mindset leads us to think we know best, without regard for God's will. As Paul says, our intellectual pride, rationalization, and excuses lead us further and further away, leaving us "hopelessly confused." Only in Christ can our hearts and minds be enlightened (Ephesians 1:18) so they are no longer darkened (Ephesians 4:18). It is only in Christ that we will truly know the love of God (Ephesians 3:17-18) and no longer live in ignorance. It is only in Christ that we have life (Ephesians 2:4-5) and are not separated from the life God gives us (Ephesians 4:18b). This is how we restore Godly sensitivity so we can know and avoid those sensualities and attractions that lead to death and shame, and we can approach the will of God which leads to life and glory.

Enlightenment is only half of the equation as Paul explains that a public transformation is necessary to demonstrate life in Christ. In verse 20, Paul draws a sharp line between the old and the new. The world should be able to see a distinction between Christians and non-Christians because we are children of light, not of darkness. Christians should walk the path of Christ in a manner all can see that there has been inner enlightenment and transformation.

Spiritual maturity is a journey, not a gift like salvation; it is a process we work toward as we grow and become more like Christ. When we accepted Him through salvation, we were marked in Christ with a seal, the promised Holy Spirit, a deposit which guarantees us our inheritance until God redeems us who are His possession to the praise of His glory (1:14). Our one-time decision leads to a daily commitment, so our transformation is both immediate and ongoing. Yes, we have the indwelling of the Holy Spirit so the old is passed away and we are made new, but we must be intentional in trusting God to continually mold and shape us into His image until our completed and final redemption when he calls us home to heaven.

We aren't mindless creatures with no responsibility or free will of our own. Quite the opposite; while God is superior in every way and we very well could be senseless beasts in service to Him, we are allowed a response in adoration to Him who has made us new. God calls us friends, not slaves, though that is what we should be. He calls us sons and daughters, so our heart's desire should be to honor Him and respond to His work with a work of our own. God calls us into relationship and partnership with Him in the maturation process so that we can be more like Christ.

Paul moves on and speaks to the integrity of this transformation as it relates to others. He is direct, almost blunt—" stop telling lies" (v.25)—as he continues his instruction. It becomes apparent in these next verses that all this talk about transformation isn't about us. We aren't in isolation.

We weren't designed to be alone or exist outside of communion with one another. God Himself is inherently relational—"Let us make humankind in our image, according to our likeness;" (Genesis 1:26), so as we are created in the image of a relational God, we too are inherently relational. The God of relationship is the God of love (1 John 4:7), but it goes so much deeper. It is not just that "God loves," but God's being is Love, a love flowing back and forth among the Father, the Son (John 17:24), and the Holy Spirit, which serves as a conduit for that love to flow through us and out to those around us. As we walk in the light, the light of that love shines for all to see, and that love becomes the motivation for all we do.

Paul stresses how we must demonstrate integrity in our relationships by being honest. In church, we are given the opportunity to speak truthfully with others, for we are each part of one body made whole in Christ. Outside of the church, we are allowed to speak truthfully to others as representatives of the body of Christ. God calls us to put on the new self, created in Christ Jesus, and speak truthfully to our neighbor.

Integrity includes not only honesty but a degree of self control. Paul also addresses an issue that we've all battled on some level at some point in our lives - anger. Note that Paul doesn't say, "Don't get angry," he says, "Don't sin by letting anger control you" (v. 26). God created human beings with emotions. We can experience emotions of love, joy, happiness, anger, fear, and jealousy, among other feelings. In the beginning, Adam and Eve were created without sin, every thought, feeling, word, and action was in alignment with God's plan for humanity. Yet, when they allowed themselves to be deceived by Satan, they fell, and every part of them - mind, body, and soul - was corrupted. Experiencing an emotion is not necessarily good or bad; it can be good when it actively brings glory to God, but it can also give way to sin, and that's where we get ourselves in trouble.

Some emotions – anger, for example – may be sinful under certain circumstances. Paul warns us in Ephesians 4:31, "Let all bitterness and wrath and anger and clamor and slander be put away from you, along with all malice." Other times, our anger may be righteous; "Be angry and do not sin; do not let the sun go down on your anger." (Ephesians 4:26). It is not the anger itself that's the problem. Instead, it is the sinful attitudes or behaviors that accompany it that are sinful. Paul recognizes that anger is reasonable and right sometimes, but we need to deal with it right away in a manner that builds rather than tears apart. If we sit in our anger, we leave ourselves vulnerable to Satan's manipulation. In such cases, instead of becoming more like Christ, our behavior reflects that of the father of lies, the devil.

When we get angry, we need to exercise a degree of self-control to maintain our integrity and outward witness of inner transformation. The first step is to identify the feeling behind it. Clinically speaking, there are three broad triggers at the root of our anger: injustice, fear, or hurt. Next, we need to be intentional and put aside our old selves, not allowing that anger to provide an excuse or even justification that would lead us to sin. Instead, we should put on our new self, surrender that anger to God, and then release it. Holding on to anger can give the devil a place to slide into our lives and antagonize our new and redeemed selves. Our goal is to be transformed by the renewing of our minds (Romans 12:2; Ephesians 4:26), not to fall back into unhealthy habits of our old nature.

Paul's straightforward warnings about the importance of integrity continue as he speaks almost as if he's addressing a classroom full of kindergarteners. "If you are a thief, quit stealing. Don't use foul or abusive language. Let everything you say be good and helpful" (v.29-29). Our morality is not conditional or situational but based on the truth of God's word. As we are transformed on the inside, we cannot help but demonstrate that transformation through our speech, our work ethic, and the way we treat others. Just as God showed His love by sending His only Son to reconcile us to Him, we too must be motivated by love.

Paul pauses his instruction here to remind us that the Holy Spirit has sealed us to guarantee that we belong to God (v. 30). The Greek word Paul uses, *esphragisthēte*, means to put a mark on an object to show possession, authority, identity, or security. We are marked for a particular purpose by the Holy Spirit's presence, living in us. But sinful behaviors bring sorrow to the Holy Spirit. We should put off our old self that would, for example, steal to get what we want. Instead, we should put on our new self, created in Christ, and use what God has given us to do something useful and worthwhile in response to God's work in us. We should earn what we have to share with others in need. The old self takes and steals; the new self earns and shares. This is the correct response to God's redemptive work in Jesus Christ that He has done in us who have heard and believed His gospel.

Discussion Questions

1. How can we be "renewed in the spirit of our mind?" (Ephesians 4:32)

2. How important is correct hearing of the gospel and faithful discipleship to shedding our old life and adopting a new way of living?

3. What connection does Paul make between sound doctrine and sanctification?

4. Consider how it grieves the Holy Spirit when we swear, lose our temper, lie, cheat, and steal. What practical steps can we follow that would enable us to have victory over habits or behaviors we know to be sinful?

5. Theologian John Stott says, "Self-control is primarily mind control." Do you agree or disagree with his statement? Why or why not?

6. Why do we need to replace our old, bad habits with new, God-honoring ones? How have you experienced this in your life?

7. Read Ephesians 4:25-32. Paul lists seven characteristics from the old self and three from the newly transformed you. Go through the list and do a self-evaluation. Are they a serious problem, an occasional struggle, or not an issue?

8. Ephesians 4:29 says to "get rid of any unwholesome talk." What are examples of the kind of talk that is negative or tears others down?

Chapter 9 - Walk This Way

Ephesians 5:1-20

Though nature has countless species that use mimicry for protection and survival, chameleons are certainly among the most fascinating of God's creations. Found primarily in the rain forests and deserts of Africa, chameleons can rearrange nanocrystals in the top layers of their skin cells to change color and blend into their habitat. The top layer of their skin is transparent, much like polar bear fur, so depending on the circumstance, they can adapt to their surroundings or threats and blend in. When triggered, the chameleon's brain sends a message to the cells to shrink or enlarge, causing specific pigments to be released, merging to create new skin tones. They not only use it to hide or to aid them in capturing prey, but they also change colors to attract a mate, regulate their body temperature, or tell predators to stay away.

Chameleons aren't the only creatures that mimic their surroundings. Humans also mimic each other. A behavior known as "The Chameleon Effect," is a phenomenon that finds us mimicking the mannerisms, gestures, or facial expressions of the people we interact with most often. It causes subconscious behavioral changes to match the behavior of people in your close social circles or even strangers. You may have observed the chameleon effect in couples who've been together for a long time or even between close friends.

Consciously or unconsciously, it is something we all do. While we might mimic a person intentionally for fun, science hasn't worked out why we subconsciously mimic others. When it happens organically, you become more relatable to the individual and easier to communicate with because they see you as someone who perceives the world in the same way they do. However, it has the opposite effect and a negative social impact when forced or manufactured. It has been said that "imitation is the sincerest form of flattery." Irish poet and playwright Oscar Wilde went a step further, quipping, "Imitation is the sincerest form of flattery that mediocrity can pay to greatness." As followers of Christ, there is no better model than Jesus Christ for how we should live out our faith in this world.

In Ephesians 5, Paul instructs us on how to mimic Jesus and become more like Him. He gives us three specific ways that we should walk in the likeness of Him: in love, in light, and in wisdom. . Even more importantly, he's going to show us where we can access the power to walk. Paul wants us to understand that as we grow in our faith and develop a deeper relationship with Jesus, we essentially experience the chameleon effect in how perfectly our lives mirror His.

Paul begins with "Therefore," because it is imperative we connect what Paul is about to say with what he has just finished saying in chapters one through four—what God has done for us in Christ, what He saved us from, and who He has predestined us to be.

In real and direct form, Paul says, "Follow God's example." What a powerful way to begin the conclusion of Ephesians. From this point forward, Paul walks us through the action steps we are to take in living out the faith he so eloquently defined for us in the first four chapters. Think of this shift as moving from objectives to tactical moves. Paul's aim at this point becomes understanding and walking by faith, spelling it out in very personal terms like submitting to one another, loving each other, and resisting sexual immorality and greed.

Following God's example means walking in the way of love as Christ did and as one of His dear children. The expression "dear children" demonstrates the expectation of the relationship. A "dear child" gladly does as their parent has requested. It also reveals the undeniable love that the Father has for us. For a Heavenly Father to say this means He has the most incredible love for us and the pride and joy of having an obedient child.

Note that Paul says we are to be followers of God because we *are* dear children, not so we can *become* dear children. That's an important distinction. Many religions teach that if you do good works, you can earn salvation and become a child of God. Christianity flips that narrative and tells us we were made a child of

God through God's grace in Christ Jesus. Paul reminded us in Ephesians 2:8-9 that our salvation is a gift of God, not the result of anything we have done. We are His children and should want to imitate Christ because we love Him.

According to Paul, we begin to walk like Christ when we walk in the way of love, just as Christ loved us. This means loving unconditionally, sacrificially, purely, without an agenda or expectation. As followers of Christ, we have two primary motivations to love. One is simply doing for others what Christ has done for us. The second is an act of love toward God—what Paul refers to as a fragrant offering (Ephesians 5:2). We are called to love everyone, as Christ loved us. He loved us while we were still unlovely and undeserving. When we love those around us, who we may view as unlovely or unworthy, it is like a fragrant offering or sacrifice before God. How would your love for others change if you looked beyond the mess to see the soul in need of a savior? If, instead of someone who wounded you or your loved ones, you saw an individual who themselves had been wounded? Jesus reminded us in Matthew 25:40 that '"whatever you did for one of the least of these brothers and sisters of mine, you did for me.'"

Not only are we to walk in love, Paul tells us we are to walk in the light. Ephesus in Paul's day was, in many ways, much like our culture today. Many people lived in spiritual darkness, pursuing happiness and satisfaction in ways that fed their baser nature and lived a life pleasing to themselves. In his typical cut-to-the-chase manner, Paul speaks directly about the hedonism common in Ephesus. He cautions us that everything that reflects that old self needs to be cast off and discarded like trash. Sexual immorality, greed, offensive speech, and covetousness must be replaced with purity, generosity, and thanksgiving. The consequences of not making such a change are dire—such a person is an idolater and has no inheritance in the kingdom of God.

Walking in the light means living a life contrary to much of what surrounds you. The world constantly tells us to speak our truth, chase the American dream, and be anything we want to be because we deserve to be happy. As a result, people spend their entire lives trying to find themselves, running from one version of themselves to the next, mirroring and mimicking all the wrong role models.

Instead, disciples of Christ know that finding our identity in anyone or anything other than Christ is futile. As we walk in His light, trying to discern what is pleasing to the Lord (Ephesians 5:8-10), we are transformed and conformed to His likeness. It is the chameleon effect in all the right ways!

Trying to discern implies intentionality in our walk. Because the light of God's love and truth illuminates our lives, there's no need to stumble around in the dark, hoping to navigate the pitfalls and traps Satan sets, or fall for one of his lies. Walking in the light takes effort because the world constantly tries to blind you to the truth. For every beautiful gift God has given us, Satan has a cheap imitation.

Canal Street in New York City's Chinatown is a major destination for finding fake designer handbags, wallets, jewelry, and other accessories. From a distance, those bags and watches may fool the casual observer, but on closer inspection, you'll see that Chanel logo actually says Channel, and your knock-off watch is probably a Rolecks, not a Rolex. Sadly, Satan uses the same tactics to cast a cloud over our vision and dupe us into thinking the things God calls sinful aren't a big deal.

Paul warns us, "Wake up, sleeper, rise from the dead, and Christ will shine on you" (Ephesians 5:14). Sin is sin, no matter how this world may try and gloss over it. When God says something is good or not good He has a reason for it and to rebel against it is sin. For instance, God's intention for sex is a far cry from how culture has warped it. God intended sex to be a profound union between a man and woman withing marriage—a co-mingling of souls. Sex within a Biblical context is an act of love and commitment where the oneness of your bodies is mirrored in the oneness in all other areas of your relationship. When you have sex outside of marriage, you take physical oneness from your partner while denying them the rest of yourself. Even if you love the other person, you haven't given yourself to him or her in covenant form.

You may say, "Well, that sounds harsh and, let's be honest, a little unreasonable. It is just sex; it is not a big deal." But look at what Paul says in verse 5: "You can be sure that no immoral, impure, or greedy person will inherit the Kingdom of Christ and of God. For a greedy person is an idolater, worshiping the things of this world." He continues in verse six, "Don't be fooled by those who try to excuse these sins, for the anger of God will fall on all who disobey him."

For those who may be feeling pretty good about themselves because they're not having sex outside marriage, note that Paul specifically calls out the greedy as well. Sin is sin, and as Paul warned us in Romans 3:23, all sin separates us from God - not just sexual sin. Our sinful nature leads us to worship whatever we think is necessary for a happy life. Greed is a craving, a constant desire for more. More power. More money. More likes on a social media post or more attention from our friends and family. Greed turns us into idolators, worshiping something other than God. A promotion. A husband. A wife. A new car, new house, a new nose. God is the only thing that can satisfy the longing of our hearts, but when you live a life of discontentment, you're saying God is not enough. There's nothing wrong with a desire to be married, excel in your career, or look and feel your best. But when those things become your overriding mission, they cross from being goals to being idols. We move from walking in the light to walking in shadow.

The third way Paul calls us to walk is in wisdom. This simply means to use godly discernment to think about things not spelled out in Scripture. For example, we sometimes wrestle with whether or not to take that promotion, marry that person, or get a job instead of heading straight to college. Walking in wisdom means we base our decisions in a manner that aligns with what God is doing in the world. Why? Because "the days are evil" (v.15), we need to be intentional about our spiritual growth. Paul takes care here to remind us that even though something may be "lawful," that is, morally good or even morally neutral, it doesn't mean it is helpful in our walk with Christ. There's nothing wrong with watching TV or spending an evening bingeing a series on Netflix. However, if what you're watching isn't "true, noble, right, pure, lovely, admirable, excellent or praiseworthy (Philippians 4:8), then we've crossed over into an area that has the potential to damage our walk with Christ.

Paul also makes a point to warn believers of the traps Satan sets for us. French poet Charles Baudelaire said, "The loveliest trick of the Devil is to persuade you that he does not exist!" It is not a stretch to say the second greatest lie is that God doesn't take sin seriously, or you can be a Christian and not be overly concerned with your lifestyle. That's a lie straight from Satan's lips. When we accept Christ as Savior, we shift from the kingdom of darkness into the kingdom of God's Son (Colossians 1:13). God moves us from spiritual darkness into the light. We can choose to go back to the dark-the devil can't make you go back, and God won't force you to stay in the light—it's a matter of free will and the difference between being righteous and being holy. We are made righteous when we accept Jesus Christ as Lord and Savior. But living in holiness is a decision of our will—what we choose to do with our life. It is your conduct—living in obedience and surrender to God's commandments.

Walking in wisdom includes discerning between truth and false assurance. Paul cautions believers against false assurances. As a Christ follower, you cannot claim Him as Savior until you surrender your will to Him as Lord, and you can't claim to be surrendered while intentionally pursuing the things that put Him on the cross. Our fallen nature means that even after salvation, we will still sin. But there's a difference between struggling with sin and dismissing it as "no big deal." Struggling means that we occasionally fall back into old habits but still repent; practicing sin means you're indifferent toward Holy Spirit conviction because Jesus isn't really your Lord.

Along with his warning against false assurances, Paul warns us of looking for false comfort. "Do not get drunk on wine, which leads to debauchery. Instead, be filled with the Spirit, (v. 18-19). What does being drunk with wine have to do with being filled with the Spirit? Both are ways of dealing with the pressures of life, but they do it in opposite ways. Alcohol is a depressant, slowing your reflexes and dulling your senses. Being filled with the Holy Spirit has the opposite effect. It sharpens your senses, gives you greater discernment, and reminds you of the hope we have in Christ. When we walk in the light, pursuing holiness, we have the peace that passes understanding and the ability to stand against temptation. Paul will discuss this later in his letter (Ephesians 6:10-18).

Walking is wisdom requires intentional action. Memorize Scripture. Meditate on it. It is not enough to sit in a service Sunday morning and listen to the preaching. We need to spend time alone with God, asking Him to reveal Himself through prayer and studying the Word. We should be engaged in small group Bible studies so others who've been where we are can encourage us, or so that we can pour into someone else who's struggling. God never intended church to be a spectator sport. It is not an event you attend but rather a community you are a part of. The blessings that come from attending church aren't the emotions that are stirred during the worship music or even from the preaching but from the Spirit of God moving through His children and pouring out into the community.

This does not discount the value of worship. Paul continues, "speaking to one another with psalms, hymns, and songs from the Spirit. Sing and make music from your heart to the Lord" (v. 18). He's not suggesting that we walk around speaking and singing only in Psalms, but that Scripture should be the soundtrack to our lives. Whether we're fighting temptation or rejoicing over God's blessings, the song in our hearts should be one of praise for all He has done, is doing, and will continue to do for us.

Discussion Questions

1.   Ephesus in Paul's day was highly secular, a city led by pagan idolators, something that could be said about much of our culture today. How do we live as "children of light" in a dark world?

2.   Some say America is a Christian country. If so, why is our society so "dark?" Do you think it is related to how the church has evolved? What about individual believers? Do you think we've failed our culture?

3.   How would your giving change if you saw it as a response to what God has done for you instead of an obligation?

4.   "Be filled with the Spirit" is a command written in the present tense. Why does Paul use a present tense verb to describe being filled with the Spirit if we receive the Holy Spirit at the moment of salvation? Why is it a command?

5.   The light metaphor speaks of Christian transparency and living joyfully in the presence of Christ, with nothing to hide or fear. As a child of light, how do you expose evil around you? How does this relate to "speaking the truth in love" (Ephesians 4:15)?

6.   Paul lists several things that can be hard for us to talk about, think about, and work on. Why is that? How might the promises Paul shares in verses 8-10 and the reminder of thanksgiving at the end of verse 4 help us with this struggle?

Chapter 10 - Spirit-Led Relationships

Ephesians 5:21-6:9

When my husband and I got engaged in 1989, I was gifted a book by a well-meaning woman in my church. It was written by the wife of a prominent pastor in the midwest at that time, and the woman who gave it to me thought it would be a handy guide for me as I, too, would be a pastor's wife in just a few months.

Bless her heart. Though parts of the book were encouraging and practical, certain sections felt like I had slipped into an alternate universe where the last 50 years had never happened. One particular chapter that is burned into my brain to this day was on personal grooming and how I should conduct myself at home. According to the author, as a wife, I was responsible for never letting my husband see me without makeup or in dirty or stained clothes. I was to get up before him in the morning, brush my teeth, put on a fresh face of makeup, style my hair, and put on a clean house dress or dressing gown over my nightgown. At the end of the day, I was to tidy the house, myself, and ensure that our children - when we had them - were also in clean clothes, fresh-faced, and ready to welcome him home from work. I should do my best to minimize noise—don't run the vacuum, dishwasher, or TV—and encourage my children to play outside or read quietly so he wouldn't be disturbed. I was to wait for him to initiate conversations and make sure I was listening to him because his topics of conversation are more important than mine.

At night, I was to go to bed in my makeup and wait to take it off after he'd fallen asleep, or at least wait until the lights were out. I was not to question his decisions, judgment, or integrity, and remember that he is the master of the house who has the right to privacy and to exercise his will with truth and fairness.

Ask my husband how often I obeyed those instructions. Actually, don't bother. The answer is never. We started dating as I was recovering from mononucleosis, so he'd already seen me without makeup multiple times. You can't make toast be bread again, and you can't unsee a face that's closer to corpse-bride than cover girl.

In these last verses in Ephesians 5 and into chapter six, Paul tackles some of the most challenging in Scripture to our 21st-century western perspective. The roles of husbands and wives inside and outside the home has evolved significantly over the past several decades as more women have entered the workforce and families have adapted to this new normal.

From a modern perspective, Paul's instructions on how wives are to submit to their husbands and slaves to their masters seem controversial and outdated, so it is imperative that Paul's words are put in first-century context. Then, we can apply his words to our lives today.

Life in the first century under Roman rule bears little resemblance to contemporary American society. Homes generally consisted of a husband, wife, children. Household slaves were also considered part of the family.. This was a male-dominated society where often women and children were little more than property. Parents arranged their children's marriages, not for love but based on what was beneficial for their families. Children submitted to their parents until they were married, in some cases even beyond, as the oldest male relative had control over extended family and married sons with their own families, including slaves. Slavery was an accepted part of Roman society, and slaves were often considered part of the family. Women regularly lived without a voice their entire lives, living under their father's authority until they were married when their submission was then to their husbands.

Before defining the roles we are to play in our relationships, Paul begins by saying, "Submit to one another out of reverence for Christ." At first, that statement sounds right and good, yet in practice, many of us chafe at the idea of submission.

Submission is arguably one of the most misunderstood concepts in Scripture, particularly when referring to a wife's submission to her husband. The idea of submission has subtle complexities beyond "do what you're told" or "because I said so." When we submit out of reverence for Christ, it becomes a matter of holiness. Submission carries such importance that it cannot be ignored or dismissed. When we submit out of reverence for Christ, it re-frames our actions to subordination to the will of our Father, just as Christ did. Submission is not synonymous with weakness. Jesus submitted to the will of His Father when He took on our sin debt and died an agonizing death on a wooden cross. Are those the actions of a weak man? Of course not. So when we submit as Jesus did, it is not from a place of weakness, but His strength.

Paul seems to make things worse when his comparison to husbands and Jesus includes the term Savior. Paul says that husbands should be head of the family as Jesus is the "head of the church, His body." But he does not stop there and continues to "of which He is the Savior." Does that suggest that the husband's body is his wife and that the husband is the Savior of his wife? No. Paul is drawing an analogy and will continue to utilize this body and savior motif to explain the husband's role and duty to his wife later in verses 25-32.

Paul understood the culture of his audience and intentionally asked women of faith to submit to their husbands. Recall how earlier we discussed that Paul did not scorn the Ephesians for their culture, but found ways to connect with them in order for them to hear the truth of the gospel. Paul knew that the

Ephesians' culture of Artemis worship sometimes led women to dominate men. As such, he had to be clear about his message. Nowhere does Paul say women are to submit to men in general, only to their own husbands. This submission gave her equal power outside the home, but a place of humility within her marriage.

So, how do we define submission between a husband and wife? Every couple is unique, so submission within each marriage will be unique to that couple. Just as day-to-day responsibilities will vary between couples, so will the way they treat each other. Volumes have been written about what submission "should" look like, but ultimately, it comes down to expectations and respect. For some couples, submission may come down to household chores; for others, sex or financial decisions. Ultimately, Paul calls on couples to open the hard dialog between a husband and wife and define what submission looks like in their relationship.They should always remember that submission is done "as unto the Lord" and out of "reverence for Christ." The keys are clarity, communication, and consistency.

Because there is no such thing as a perfect husband, submission involves a level of risk. How can a wife know he is making the right choices for the family? The bottom line is that she won't always be able to discern that. Scripture is clear; the wife is called to submit. It would be understandable to think this is unreasonable and unfair. However,Paul allows space and room for growth and change. Nothing stays the same, so areas of submission will change over time.

At this point, it would appear that the husband has the more privileged or entitled role but that's not the case. Paul instructs, "Husbands, love your wives, just as Christ loved the Church." God has placed a much heavier load on the shoulders of the husband. His position puts him under scrutiny as He will give an account to God for all he does in his family. His heightened scrutiny comes because he is to be head of the home just as Christ is head of the Church. When you consider the weight of that comparison, you see that God will deal with him if he is not following His direction as an example to his family.

There is considerable debate within many churches today regarding the roles of women. Complementarianism and Egalitarianism are opposing theological positions on the relationship between men and women, especially within marriage and in ministry. Egalitarians assert that there are no gender distinctions in roles. Because we are all one in Christ, men and women are interchangeable when it comes to the functional roles of leadership in the home and the church. Complementarians believe in the essential equality of men and women as persons created in God's image. However, they believe some roles are gender specific when it comes to functional roles in society, the church, and the home.

Ultimately, those who hold an egalitarian position often fail to understand that the differentiation in roles does not equate to a difference in quality, importance, or value. Men and women hold equal value in God's sight and plan. Both are created in the image of God, and women are in no way inferior to men. Instead, God designates different roles for men and women because that is how He designed us to function.

The Trinity perfectly illustrates this functional complementation (1 Corinthians 11:3). Jesus, the Son, submits to His Father, and the Holy Spirit submits to the Father and the Son. This functional submission does not imply inferiority; all three Persons are equally God, but each differs in their function. In the same way, men and women are equally human and created in God's image, but each has God-ordained roles and responsibilities that parallel the functional complementation within the Trinity.

Now that we understand Biblical submission for women, we see that "wives submit to their husbands as to the Lord" is no longer the oppressive, servile position that some have interpreted it to be.

Perhaps the the more often overlooked question is, what does "love your wife" as Christ loved the Church mean?

A husband who truly loves his wife as Christ loves the Church is a man of initiative and action. 1 John 4:19 says, "We love because He first loved us." So a husband who loves his wife as Christ loves the Church is a man who will be intentional in showing his wife love. He will always forgive, not hold grudges, and treat his wife with respect, offering grace and compassion whenever it is needed. A woman loved by such a man will never feel insecure in the relationship because she knows he loves her above all others. She is a priority and his precious bride. A husband who loves his wife like Christ loved the Church is always ready to repair, reconcile and restore the relationship when required.

The love Jesus demonstrated on earth is the standard of love that husbands should have for their wives. Jesus left heaven to be humbled and born human yet still fully God. He loved so deeply that he lived a ministry of homelessness and rejection, was mercilessly and savagely scourged in the hours leading to His crucifixion, and then died an excruciating and humiliating death. Furthermore, He did it all to take on the full wrath of God for our rebellion. The fruit of this infinite work was for the Church to be made holy, the cleansing that comes by the washing with water through the word.

We are His bride, holy and clean, shining in the perfection that Jesus suffered for us to have. The love demonstrated in such action is the standard of love that husbands should have for their wives. This is what it means to be the head of the wife.

Not only is the husband to sacrifice for his wife, but he is also to treat his wife with love. In his book Love & Respect: The Love She Most Desires; The Respect He Desperately Needs, Dr. Emerson Eggerichs says it is imperative to understand that communication between a husband and wife involves understanding one thing: unconditional respect is as powerful for a man as unconditional love is for a woman. Although both men and women deserve love and respect in equal measure when conflict arises within a marriage, a man's primary need is respect, and a woman's is love. If either of these needs isn't met, conflict erupts and escalates.

Because a husband and wife become one flesh, they are one in all things. God made them one flesh, but the Fall left them divided, resulting in sin and its curse. Paul addresses the curse of women and what happened in the Garden of Eden. The Fall of mankind meant that a woman would have pain in childbirth and desire to dominate her husband. This conflict between husbands and wives is as old as Adam and Eve. When a relationship falls apart, it reminds us of the Fall of mankind and the departure from God's plan for a husband and wife.

One of the most challenging concepts Paul discusses in this section is cleansing and holiness as a part of the marriage. The husband is called to be the "spiritual leader of the home," yet sadly, many men are not as interested in spiritual matters. They tend to leave issues of faith to their wife. This is backward. Cleansing and holiness involve spiritual disciplines, including reading the Bible, praying, bringing your family to church, and leading them to be like Christ. This is not to be ignored, and men who leave matters of faith to their wives do so at their peril.

Paul continues with instructions on the relationship between parents and children. Don't overlook the significance of children being addressed in this passage. Paul takes time to instruct children, demonstrating that they were part of the early church. This may seem an insignificant detail, but when we consider that Jesus talked to children and used them in His sermons, we see He highly valued them and their ability to experience faith.

Paul addresses children with an Old Testament Commandment familiar to Jewish believers. They are to honor their father and mother, a commandment with the promise of long life (Deuteronomy 5:16). Other commandments are to be obeyed as God's expectation; obedience to this commandment comes with a reward.

To what degree should parents be obeyed? What if a parent commands their child to do something contrary to the law of Christ? Paul clarifies this command by saying, "obey your parents *in the Lord*." Our obedience is to be firmly rooted "in Christ" because His will is primary, and we are not to depart from it. The child that follows this teaching and remembers that he or she belongs to the Lord will have peace at home. He or she will have the favor of the Lord. Obedience isn't difficult when our actions are motivated by love.

The dynamic between fathers and their children, especially sons, is critical to the parent/child relationship. An abrasive, authoritarian father will cultivate an angry child. Paul uses evocative language in these verses, warning fathers against an aggressive parenting style, saying, "do not provoke your children to anger." Some translations use the word "exasperate" rather than provoke and "wrath" rather than anger. You can feel the tension in Paul's words.

This passage may shed a little light on Paul's personal experience with relationships I mentioned Paul had when we started this chapter. The focus of these words makes one wonder about Paul's home life as a child that he would make a statement about this. We learn through the Bible of the hardship he endured throughout his ministry, his strict adherence to Pharisaical rules and laws, and his perfectionism. Add in on top of all this the overtly encouraging self-talk in his writings, and it gives the impression Paul might have had first-hand experience with the frustration of living with a demanding father.

Discipline and instruction are part of a father or mother's duty, but they must be based on Biblical wisdom that can only be discerned through a close walk with the Lord. Therefore, parents must cultivate their relationship with the Lord as well as with each other. Understanding that our children ultimately belong to the Lord and we are only channels for the work He will do in that young life gives us the perspective we need to parent with wisdom and compassion.

Finally, Paul addresses the relationship between slaves and masters. As always, historical and cultural context is vital. Slavery in America during the 18th and 19th centuries differed from slavery in the Roman Empire. Scripture condemns the slavery found in America, where men, women, and children were stolen, sold, and forced into slavery (Deuteronomy 24:7). In the Roman Empire, enslaved people had some legal rights. However, they lacked honor and were subject to whatever punishments their masters deemed appropriate. They were not allowed to own property and could be separated from their spouse if their master chose.

We may be tempted to skip these verses and assume they are irrelevant to us today. However, consider how these instructions compare in context to the modern day employment scenario. God gave specific instructions on how slaves and masters should conduct themselves, a relationship where one party holds all the power. How much more do these instructions apply to us and the employer/employee relationship?

First, Paul says we are to serve as though we are serving Jesus (v.5, 7). We are to obey those who have authority over us on this earth, meaning we will serve wholeheartedly and with the right spirit as though our work is for Jesus Himself. Paul gives no allowance for slacking off or doing poor work if we have a terrible boss. Instead, we are to do our job with determination, obedience, and serving from our heart as an expression of our commitment to the Lord. We may be paid by man, but our work is for God Himself.

Paul also instructs us to work with integrity (v. 6). We're not only to work when the boss is looking, but also to work when the boss is not watching. Someone is always watching, whether it is corporate or a coworker, and our testimony can be negatively impacted if we're constantly slacking off or demonstrating a lack of integrity in our work. Paul reminds us in verse 8 that we'll be rewarded for our good work. Think of the slaves serving, unjustly taken advantage of every day, without the freedom or ability to change their circumstances. No wonder so many tried to run away. We may feel a measure of injustice if our supervisor or boss takes advantage of us, but Paul reminds us that God sees, God knows, and God will reward us.

Finally, Paul instructs masters—or bosses—to remember that, though they may have authority over others here on earth, we are all equal in God's sight. Paul's letter to Philemon stresses this. Philemon, the master, and Onesimus, his slave, were brothers in Christ. Therefore, if you're in a position of authority over a team or staff, you are to treat them respectfully and remember that you are not the ultimate authority—God is.

Discussion Questions

1. Men and women have equal value, but they also have different roles. How did God design men and women differently? How do these differences complement each other?

2. Do you take a complementarian or egalitarian approach to the roles of men and women in the home and in the church? Why? Does Scripture support your position?.

3. How does Paul's illustration regarding the relationship between Christ and the church shape the way husbands and wives relate?

4. Why does Paul single out fathers in verse four? Does this instruction apply to both parents?

5. Do you think Paul's character was shaped by an authoritarian father?

6. We have two primary motivations at work: love for Jesus and a desire to show the world our love for him through how we work. How does that play out in your workplace?

7. Read Exodus 20:12, which Paul cites in verses two and three. How does "honor" relate to "obedience?"

Chapter 11 - Suit Up!

Ephesians 6:10-24

Pizza and body armor aren't two things that often appear in the same sentence, but thanks to inventor Richard Davis, one is inextricably connected to the other. After completing his service in the U.S. Marine Corps, Richard Davis opened a pizzeria off 7 Mile in Detroit. Late one night, a delivery took him through a back alley and he was held up at gunpoint. A couple of weeks later on another delivery to the same address, he was shot in another attempted robbery. This time around, Davis had hidden a .22 revolver under the pizzas and he returned fire, wounding two of his three attackers. Davis himself was shot, and in the weeks he spent recovering, his pizzeria was burned to the ground.

Some men might have thought this would be an excellent time to get a nice quiet office job or jump on the assembly line at Ford, but Davis had other ideas. While he was recovering, eight police officers were shot in unrelated incidents over a single weekend across the United States. Davis felt that most of the officers could have survived if they had been wearing proper protection. He'd heard about a breakthrough in tire technology over at DuPont Co. Labs, where researchers had developed a new, lightweight, super-strong synthetic fabric called Kevlar, reportedly five-times stronger than steel. Davis managed to get his hands on some of the Kevlar, and using an awl, a pair of scissors, and a roll of ballistic nylon, he fabricated a body armor vest. He wanted it to be lightweight, flexible, and comfortable enough to be worn an entire shift. It was also vital that it be able to be worn under clothing because his theory was that if the assailant could see the vest, they'd simply shoot an unprotected area.

Davis spent his days fabricating vests and his nights trying to convince local police to buy them. Though they appreciated what Davis had to say, it was untested on a person so they were reluctant to purchase them. Finally, Davis decided it was time to prove the efficacy of his "Second Chance Vest," so he gathered a group of police to watch a demonstration where he announced he was going to shoot himself in the chest. He wasn't kidding.

Davis pulled the trigger on himself, and while the vest couldn't stop inertia, it did stop the bullet. He was left with broken skin, and later a wicked bruise, but the officers were sold. For a mere $50 a vest, police officers were willing to pay out of their own pockets on the spot. The demonstration and the vest's power to save a life was so effective, it eventually became standard among police departments across the country. To this day, law enforcement and troops around the world wear variations of Davis' Second Chance Vest.

Paul concludes his letter to the Ephesians outlining how they can suit up with protection. Think of it as spiritual kevlar. Paul starts by reviewing all he's taught up to now. He lays out the nature of the spiritual battle we face every day and describes how we can find the strength to resist temptations. Then he pleads with the Ephesians to cover themselves with prayer because prayer is one the most powerful weapons in our arsenal.

The age we now live in here on earth is bookended by two advents of Christ. At His first coming, Jesus defeated sin and now has dominion and authority over all creation (Ephesians 1:20-21). When He returns, Jesus will conquer sin and Satan once and for all, delivering us from evil for all eternity. Until then, the battle rages around us (1 Peter 5:8), and we must suit up with the armor and weapons God has provided for His church.

Paul uses two passages from Isaiah to illustrate how we as believers can be equipped for spiritual warfare (Isaiah 11:1-5; 59:17-20). The illustration would have been familiar to Jewish believers yet easy for the Gentiles to understand as well. In Paul's day, there was no better example of military strength than the mighty Roman army. At its peak, the Roman empire encompassed 2.5 million square miles and spanned three continents: Asia, Africa, and Europe. Its near-global conquest was made possible by its army—one of the most successful in the history of the world. Roman soldiers were feared for their training, discipline, and stamina, which brought them great victory on the battlefield. There was no better illustration for Paul's audience.

But a second, more important application of these verses from Isaiah is that the descriptions are of Christ. Paul applies those descriptions to the Ephesians. He explains that because we are God's workmanship (Ephesians 2:10), members of His household (Ephesians 2:19), and parts of Christ's body (Ephesians 4:16), Christ invites us to put on His armor in order to protect ourselves in spiritual warfare.

Paul starts with the belt of truth. Every Roman soldier wore at least one wide belt under his armor. The belt held his clothing together, prevented his armor from digging into his flesh, protected the lower abdomen, and was used to sheath the soldier's sword. Paul uses the soldier's belt as an illustration of truth. In Ephesians 4:25, Paul cautioned that we must "put off falsehood and speak truthfully" and in Ephesians 5:9, he tells us the fruit of godliness "consists in all goodness, righteousness, and truth." Paul wants us to understand that lies, duplicity, and deceit give the devil a foothold in our lives that can only lead to destruction.

Next, Paul tells us we are to put on the breastplate of righteousness. Much like Davis' body armor vest, Paul sees the necessity of protecting our most vulnerable organ - our heart. What is our protection? Righteousness. This is two-fold. First, we have been made righteous by Christ's death on our behalf (imputed righteousness). We are "holy," "set apart," and "saints" who belong to God from the moment of salvation. His righteousness is our righteousness because His blood covers our sins. And His imputed righteousness must be accompanied by living holy lives in obedience and walking in God's ways. Paul warned us in Ephesians 4:25-5:7 to put off sins like malice, slander, bitterness, sexual immorality, and anger, and instead put on kindness, compassion, and gratitude. Paul understood that Satan targets our hearts, and even the most faithful disciples could fall for Satan's tricks if they aren't diligently protecting their hearts. Satan prowls the earth like a roaring lion looking for someone to devour (1 Peter 5:8), and without the breastplate of righteousness, we are easy marks.

The armor includes a component of readiness as well. Isaiah 52:7 sheds light on what Paul refers to when he tells us our feet should be "shod with the readiness that comes from the gospel." Isaiah says, "How beautiful...are the feet of those who bring good news, who proclaim peace...who proclaim salvation." Rather than bringing conflict or forcing conquered peoples to surrender to the tyranny of Rome, believers should bring hope and peace by proclaiming the gospel of Jesus Christ. Paul demonstrates his own willingness later in Ephesians 6:19-20, where he asks for prayer so that he might "fearlessly make known the mystery of the gospel."

Paul then tells us we are to arm ourselves with the shield of faith. Roman shields were made by gluing multiple layers of wood together. Though durable and practical, the problem was their vulnerability to water.

To avoid warp and rot, shield makers stretched a piece of tanned leather across the shield to protect it, not increasing its lifespan but making it even more impervious to weapons. Additionally, during battle, soldiers would often wrap their shields with strips of wet linen to absorb fiery arrows and prevent further damage.

Paul compares the flaming arrows of Rome's enemies to the way Satan attacks us with lies and deceit. He spent the first two chapters of Ephesians describing all that is true about us who are in Christ, yet Satan uses every weapon in his arsenal - lies, half-truths, false promises, accusations - to warp what we know to be true about who God is and what we have in Him. Unless we protect ourselves with the shield of faith to quench and deflect those attacks, we're helpless against him. Instead of falling in battle, we can stand firm and fend off the attack through the truth of God's word. This is why Scripture memory is vitally important to the believer.

Whether you're riding your bike to school or marching into battle against the entire Trojan army, helmets save lives. Paul reminds us that our salvation serves as a spiritual helmet, protecting us against self-doubt and the fear that God will turn his back on us when we fail. Instead, we must place our confidence in Him, remembering our salvation is a gift from God. We are secure because the work was done by Him, not by anything we have done. (Ephesians 2:8-9).

The final piece of our armor is the sword of truth. Note that all the weapons Paul mentions are primarily defensive, except one—God's word, which is both defensive and offensive. We counter the enemy's blows with our sword and thrust home when we see a weakness in his defense.

Our sword is God's Word. The single most effective weapon we have against the attacks of our enemy is Scripture itself. Jesus Himself answered Satan's temptations and lies with passages from the Old Testament (Luke 4:1-13) during the 40 days he spent in the wilderness. Bible study, meditating, and memorizing passages of Scripture keep us sharp, so when the devil attacks, and he will, we're prepared.

What's important to remember about this passage is that each piece of armor is crucial. If even one part is missing, we are vulnerable to our enemy. Just as a soldier knows to attack their enemy's weakest point, so Satan knows exactly where you are most exposed and easily defeated.

Paul illustrates three powerful truths in these verses. One, we are engaged in spiritual warfare between the powers of darkness and the power of God. Looking at the problems of the world from a strictly human vantage point ignores the very real presence of Satan and his demons actively working against the kingdom of God every day. Two, while merely "standing our ground" may not seem like a victory, any time you stand your ground against Satan is indeed a victory. When we give in to temptation, we fall back or, to use an old church-speak term, "backslide." However, when we stand firm, we defeat the devil (James 4:7) and strengthen our character. Finally, never forget that Satan is a schemer. This is the same being known as Lucifer, the angel of light, that was cast out of heaven for mounting a rebellion against God. The prophet Ezekiel describes Lucifer prior to his fall as "the model of perfection, full of wisdom and exquisite in beauty." But his beauty was his downfall. His name Lucifer translates to "day star," but once he was cast from heaven, God changed his name to Satan, meaning "adversary." He's clever and never doubt that he can be convincing; Revelation 12:3-4 tells us he "swept a third of the stars from heaven." Those "stars" are angels who were captivated by his lies and false promises. If angels who dwelt in the presence of God Himself can be deceived, how can we ever be so vain to think ourselves immune to his fiendish charm?

The battle won't be over until Jesus comes again, but don't be discouraged or overcome by fear. God has given us everything we need to win this war. By believing Him, placing our trust in Him, obeying Him, and relying on His strength, we will be victorious.

In verse 18, Paul transitions from his military analogy to exhorting the Ephesians to pray. He encourages us to pray throughout each day as we encounter temptations and to pause and pray in gratitude for God's goodness and blessings. There are many examples in Scripture, but one of my favorites is Nehemiah. When he heard about his fellow citizen's peril and Jerusalem's dire situation, Nehemiah immediately stopped to pray a long and passionate prayer, pouring his heart out to God. Later, when he stood before the throne, Nehemiah uttered a quick prayer before speaking to King Artaxerxes I. Prayer was an integral part of Nehemiah's lifestyle, as natural as breathing, as it should be part of ours.

Paul also encouraged the Ephesians to pray in the Spirit, according to God's will, not our own, in submission to Him. Prayer shouldn't be a litany of demands but rather humbly coming before God seeking His will. Prayer is an opportunity to align our heart's with our Father's, rather than trying to convince Him to give in to our demands. Paul challenges us to be alert, unlike the disciples who fell asleep the night before Jesus was crucified. We must be attentive to what the enemy is up to and his readiness to exploit our weakness.

We're also to pray with perseverance. God isn't a genie in a lamp, waiting to grant us wishes on demand. Instead, He wants us to come to Him with all our requests, but His timing isn't always our timing. Bring those requests to Him again and again until he answers yes, no, or not now. Unless you're persistent, you may miss His answer.

Praying for one another is critical to the spiritual health and growth of the believer. It is easy to fall into a pattern of asking for things for ourselves. Even when we're praying for others, there's sometimes a selfish motive behind our prayers. But Paul reminds us we need to focus on others. We're in a spiritual battle, and prayer is one of the most effective weapons we can use to defeat the devil. Praying for others is one of the most powerful ways of serving others.

Paul closes his petition by asking the Ephesians to pray for him. But rather than asking them to pray for his impending trial, better living conditions, or even to be released, he asks for boldness in sharing the gospel. How often do our prayers focus on our physical needs? There's nothing wrong with asking God to help you use your money wisely, for good health, or for success at work. But if most of your prayer life focuses on physical rather than spiritual needs, it is time to evaluate where your heart's desire truly lies.

As his letter to the Ephesians concludes, Paul finishes with a blessing and a benediction (v. 21-24). He promises to send Tychicus, his beloved brother and faithful minister in the Lord (Acts 20:4). Tychicus is mentioned in five New Testament books (Acts, Ephesians, Colossians, 2 Timothy, and Titus). He accompanied Paul on his third missionary journey to Jerusalem. Few people would have better insight into Paul's physical, spiritual and mental health than a man who had walked beside him through so many trials and tribulations. Paul is confident that the Christ-followers in Ephesus will be encouraged when they hear about how and what he is doing, saying, "So that you also may know how I am and what I am doing..." (v. 21), and "I have sent him to you for this very purpose, that you may know how we are..." (v. 22).

Never one to shy away from the truth, Paul hides nothing from the believers in Ephesus. Just as he encouraged young Timothy in 1 Timothy 4:12 to "...set believers an example in speech, in conduct, in love, in faith, in purity," Paul instructs Tychicus to tell them everything (v.21). What a beautiful example of authentic Christianity. No doubt Paul had highs and lows, good days and bad, and moments he questioned why God would allow him to be imprisoned. But, understanding how vital transparency is among believers, Paul told Timothy, "Practice these things, immerse yourself in them, so that all may see your progress. Keep a close watch on yourself and on the teaching. Persist in this, for by so doing you will save both yourself and your hearers" (1 Timothy 4:15-16).

In his final benediction, Paul wishes the the Ephesians peace , that they love with faith from God and Jesus Christ, both the source and the object of our faith. Even incarcerated, Paul never loses sight of his calling (2 Timothy 3:10). He remained faithful, and he proved to be a faithful steward of the ministry to which he had been called (1 Corinthians 4:2).

We love because God first loved us; we know peace because He gives us peace; we have grace because He is gracious. Paul wishes grace for all believers and love incorruptible, perhaps better translated as "undying love," the kind every Christian should have toward Christ. This Greek word for love is used only a handful of times in the New Testament, usually in conjunction with the resurrection (Romans 2:7; 1 Corinthians 15:42; 2 Timothy 1:10). This is the abiding, unfailing love for Christ that marks His true disciples and sets us apart from what might be called a merely cultural Christianity. Paul wants the Ephesians to know the unknowable love of Christ (3.19) because when we know His love, our love for Him will grow deeper.

Discussion Questions

1. In verses 11 and 13, Paul encourages us to "put on the full armor of God." Compare this to words spoken about Christ in Isaiah 59:16-17. What can we learn by comparing these passages?

2. Can you think of an example from your own life, or from the lives of others, when you/they didn't put on the whole armor of God? What was the result?

3. The Greek word for "struggle" in verse 12 (palē) translates to "wrestling match." How does this change your understanding of this verse?

4. Consider the armor Paul tells us to put on. Give practical examples of how to use each of the pieces listed.

5. Notice the irony that Paul is "an ambassador" of the Lord of lords, but yet "in chains." Do you think his imprisonment undermined his message, or did it make it more powerful?

6. Is declaring the gospel fearlessly the same as declaring the gospel bluntly? What about those who have theological arguments on social media? Do you think this is an effective way to share the gospel, or does it do more harm than good?

Conclusion

Ephesus in Paul's day was culturally chaotic, heavily influenced by the occult, and ruled by those vehemently opposed to Paul's ministry. Yet, Paul loved the people and had a commitment to the mission God gave to him of sharing the good news of the gospel with the Gentiles. This meant he was an encouragement and blessing even from a Roman prison.

Throughout his epistle, Paul encouraged and poured love into the believers in Ephesus because he wanted them to be rooted and grounded in love. He desired that they would allow God to guide them so they could model how to live in community and harmony. Beginning with the foundational truth that salvation is a gift from God, not because of anything we could ever do to earn it, Paul strengthened their faith and encouraged them to strive for spiritual maturity. He reminded them that through His finished work on the cross, Jesus Christ redeemed and sealed us, setting us apart from the world. Furthermore, God's love covers all believers with grace and mercy. All believers means Jews and Gentiles alike - the gospel is for all people of every nation, tribe, and tongue.

Contrary to what many Jews thought, God intended to save all humanity, not just the Jews; this is the mystery of God. Through Christ, Jews and Gentiles are unified as sons and daughters of God, adopted into His family with all the rights and privileges of natural-born children. God wants us to be complete in Him, body, soul, and spirit.

Believer, never forget there is an ongoing battle between good and evil happening all around you, every day, between the kingdom of God and the kingdom of darkness. Satan and his demons wage war against us; they possess great power and ability and know your weaknesses better than you do.

But, don't be fearful or discouraged because God has given us the victory. As Paul tells us in 1 Corinthians 15:57, "But thanks be to God! He gives us the victory through our Lord Jesus Christ." How is this victory possible? Because of the finished work of Jesus, the One who died for our sins, was buried, and rose from the dead, according to the Scriptures. Satan's malignant fury that warped the minds of the men and women who put Jesus on the cross was his downfall. We have victory because God has equipped us with every weapon we need to defeat the devil and wage a counterattack. When we suit up in the full armor of God, we can quench Satan's fiery arrows and protect ourselves from every spear and sword with the shield of faith.

Most importantly, we have the ultimate weapon against which Satan cannot stand - the Sword of the Spirit, which is the Word of God. God never promised the believer a peaceful life of ease - those are lies the devil tells to dupe the unsuspecting into following him. But God has promised to strengthen us with grace and truth, so we too can be victorious over sin. Paul reminds us we are "more than conquerors through him that loved us" in Romans 8:37. Nothing can separate us from the love of God in Christ.

The One who has defeated death and the grave gives us the victory. Ask Him to do far more abundantly than we could ask or think according to that immeasurably great power. What was hidden is now revealed, and the Son of Man now sits at the right hand of the Father in power and majesty.

Now to him who is able to do immeasurably more than all we ask or imagine, according to his power that is at work within us, to him be glory in the Church and in Christ Jesus throughout all generations, forever and ever! Amen (Ephesians 3:21).

Acknowledgments

It's been said that writing a book is like having a baby. I'm not sure who decided that, but I'm confident it wasn't a woman, and certainly not a woman who's actually had a baby. I understand where they're coming from - the creative process can be arduous - but ultimately, creating a cohesive narrative is a far cry from creating life.

To me, writing a book is more like starting a relationship. You're excited but apprehensive, ready to see where things lead but guarded in case it goes sideways, somewhat confident you know what you're doing yet painfully aware of how much work it will take to create something worthwhile. Both take a level of vulnerability, something that can be intimidating.

My name may be on the cover, but writing this book would not have been possible without the skills, encouragement, and support of so many people in my life.

I dedicated this book to my husband Roy not just because he's my best friend but because he has been integral to this process. He's my biggest cheerleader and makes me laugh harder than anyone else I know. That may seem unrelated to writing this book, but trust me, when you're deep in the weeds and think you're in over your head, you need someone like Roy in your corner, leading you out and making you laugh along the way. His theological knowledge and his training and experience as a licensed therapist were integral to ensuring the content of this book is both doctrinally and clinically sound.

Thank you to my pastor and friend, Christian Gaffney, whose personal study notes are the foundation of this work. This book was Christian's idea, and his confidence in me to adapt some of his notes into a study to accompany his Ephesians sermon series is humbling. Our families have been blessed to serve in ministry together for many years, and much of who my daughters are today is a result of Christian and his wife Stephanie's influence on their lives. His deep understanding of Scripture and ability to transform complex theology into practical applications for daily living never ceases to amaze me. Christian patiently read every word of every draft I shared with him and painstakingly edited, proofed, and elevated this work.

Thank you to my daughters Ceilidh and Sarah and to my son-in-law Nikko who cheered me on from the sidelines, made me tea, and sometimes dinner, so I could keep working.

Thank you to my proofreaders, Trent Kirkland, Shannon Baccaglini, Kristina Smith, Tanya Mac Lean, and Rachel Rock. Thank you for taking the time out of your busy schedules to read the manuscript and offer edits, encouragement, and practical suggestions. Your diverse life experiences and careers - pastor, Director of Data Integrity and Quality - Analyst in Organizational Change Management - what even do those words mean? - purchasing manager, and police officer - made the book accessible to a broader range of readers.

Special thanks to Danielle Waterfield, who spent long hours into the night and early mornings to develop this manuscript into the book you hold today. Through the same laser-sharp precision she uses to write legal briefs, Danielle took my manuscript and made it more precise, concise, and reader-friendly.

Thank you to Mike Zizolfo, who created the cover art for this book and the sermon series it accompanies. I don't know how you do what you do, but you do it well - your work is brilliant.

Thank you to my ministry team coworkers Roy Dowdy, Sarah Custodio, and Brenda Boose. You helped me balance my responsibilities within the team against writing this book, especially in the last weeks of this project.

Finally, thank you to my parents, Brian and Sally Mac Lean, whose lifelong love of reading made me the book nerd I am today. My earliest memories are of bedtime stories, a tradition I carried on with my own children. My parents demonstrated a lifelong love of learning, love for one another, and a deep commitment to serving Jesus. Your example is on every page of this book. Thank you.

Sources

Adam Hughes | March 6, 2020. (2020, March 6). *The themes of Ephesians*. The Themes of Ephesians. Retrieved August 17, 2022, from https://preachingsource.com/blog/the-themes-of-ephesians/

Ashby, C. (2022, March 29). *Crime and punishment*. Life in the Roman Empire: Historical Fact and Fiction . Retrieved August 17, 2022, from https://carolashby.com/crime-and-punishment-in-the-roman-empire/

Chartrand, T. L., & Bargh, J. A. (1999). The chameleon effect: The perception–behavior link and social interaction. *Journal of Personality and Social Psychology, 76*(6), 893–910. https://doi.org/10.1037/0022-3514.76.6.893

Foulkes, F. (2015). *Ephesians: An introduction and commentary*. Inter-Varsity Press.

Furman, G. (2017). *Alive in him: How being embraced by the love of christ changes everything*. Crossway.

Giving thanks can make you happier. Harvard Health. (2021, August 14). Retrieved September 7, 2022, from https://www.health.harvard.edu/healthbeat/giving-thanks-can-make-you-happier#:~:text=In%20positive%20psychology%20research%2C%20gratitude,adversity%2C%20and%20build%20strong%20relationships.

Heck, S. (2020, November 19). *How to speak the truth in Love*. How to Speak the Truth in Love. Retrieved September 7, 2022, from https://biblicalcounseling.com/resource-library/articles/how-to-speak-the-truth-in-love/

History.com Editors. (2018, February 2). *Ephesus*. History.com. Retrieved September 7, 2022, from https://www.history.com/topics/ancient-greece/ephesus#:~:text=Ephesus%20is%20mentioned%20multiple%20times,open%20to%20Paul's%20Christian%20message.

JA;, C. T. L. B. (1999, November 6). *The chameleon effect: The perception-behavior link and Social Interaction*. Journal of personality and social psychology. Retrieved August 7, 2022, from https://pubmed.ncbi.nlm.nih.gov/10402679/

Jeremiah, D. (2022, May 17). *Who is Lucifer in the Bible?* David Jeremiah Blog. Retrieved August 10,

2022, from https://davidjeremiah.blog/who-is-lucifer/

Köstenberger Andreas J., & Jones, D. W. (2010). *God, marriage, and Family: Rebuilding the biblical foundation.* Crossway.

LUCADO, M. A. X. (2018). *Life lessons from ephesians;where you belong.* HARPERCHRISTIAN RESOURCES.

McRay, J. (1995, July 1). *Stench, pain, and misery.* Christian History | Learn the History of Christianity & the Church. Retrieved September 7, 2022, from https://www.christianitytoday.com/history/issues/issue-47/stench-pain-and-misery.html

Mosier, K. (2021, October 7). *What am I feeling? shame or conviction?* Cornerstone Christian Counseling. Retrieved September 7, 2022, from https://christiancounselingco.com/what-am-i-feeling-shame-or-conviction/

National Geographic . (2014, July 1). *About the Mariana Trench - Deepsea Challenge Expedition.* DEEPSEA CHALLENGE. Retrieved September 7, 2022, from http://www.deepseachallenge.com/the-expedition/mariana-trench/

National Geographic. (n.d.). *Chameleon.* Animals. Retrieved September 7, 2022, from https://kids.nationalgeographic.com/animals/reptiles/facts/chameleon

Piper, J. (2005). *Taste and see: 140 meditations*. Multnomah Publishers.

Redmond, E. C. (2016). *Ephesians: A 12-week study*. Crossway Books.

Wright, N. T., & Johnson, L. (2009). *Ephesians: 11 studies for individuals and groups*. IVP Connect.

Yirka, B. (2021, July 13). Oldest known cosmetics found in ceramic bottles on Balkan Peninsula. Retrieved September 7, 2022, from https://phys.org/news/2021-07-oldest-cosmetics-ceramic-bottles-balkan.html

Zondervan. (2011). *Niv Life Application Study Bible*.